CLIFFS COURSE OUTLINES

American Government

by

RICHARD C. RATLIFF, PH.D.

CLIFFS NOTES, INC. • LINCOLN, NEBRASKA 68501

To my patient wife, Dottie, who keeps the house quiet during working hours, and to the many students who have indicated the need for such a work, this course outline is—with deep appreciation—dedicated.

ISBN   0-8220-1525-0

© Copyright 1973

by

CLIFFS NOTES, INC.

Foreword

This Course Outline represents a condensation of the material generally offered in college survey courses commonly titled American Government, American National Government, or American Federal Government. Its design is based on the author's 22 years as a college teacher, and its general organization is intended to parallel the characteristics of organization found common to the leading conventional textbooks which have won broad adoption for the basic course in American Government. In those instances where a major difference of structure has occurred between the leading conventional textbooks, some effort has been made to swing the outline wide enough to be inclusive, rather than restrictive. In other instances, the author has included materials which he has found useful to his students, but which are commonly overlooked by textbooks.

The student is reminded that this outline is not expected to take the place of the assigned textbook, but is intended as a supplement to textbook and lecture materials. Since all study of American Government has a certain direct relationship to an understanding of the Constitution of the United States, it is suggested that the student enter this Course Outline through a study of the outline and the text of the Constitution which are presented in the Appendixes near the back of the book.

It is perhaps appropriate, too, to remind the student in the beginning that the study of government is largely concerned with the study of power and the use of power to regulate individuals in a common society.

List of Textbooks Keyed to Outline

ADRIAN, CHARLES R., and CHARLES PRESS. *The American Political Process.* Second edition. New York: McGraw-Hill Book Company, 1969.

BURNS, JAMES MACGREGOR, and J. W. PELTASON. *Government by the People.* Eighth edition. Englewood Cliffs, N. J.: Prentice-Hall, Inc., 1972.

CARR, ROBERT K., MARVER H. BERNSTEIN, WALTER F. MURPHY, and MICHAEL N. DANIELSON. *American Democracy.* Sixth edition. New York: Holt, Rinehart and Winston, Inc., 1971.

CUMMINGS, MILTON C., JR., and DAVID WISE. *Democracy Under Pressure.* New York: Harcourt Brace Jovanovich, Inc., 1971.

DAHL, ROBERT A. *Democracy in the United States: Promise and Performance.* Second edition. Chicago: Rand McNally & Company, 1972.

DIAMOND, MARTIN, WINSTON MILLS FISK, and HERBERT GARFINKEL. *The Democratic Republic.* Second edition. Rand McNally & Company, 1970.

EBENSTEIN, WILLIAM, C. HERMAN PRITCHETT, HENRY A. TURNER, and DEAN MANN. *American Democracy in World Perspective.* Second edition. New York: Harper & Row, Publishers, 1970.

FERGUSON, JOHN H., and DEAN E. MCHENRY. *The American Federal Government.* Eleventh edition. New York: McGraw-Hill Book Company, 1971.

IRISH, MARIAN D., and JAMES W. PROTHRO. *The Politics of American Democracy.* Fifth edition. Englewood Cliffs, N. J.: Prentice-Hall, Inc., 1971.

NIMMO, DAN, and THOMAS D. UNGS. *American Political Patterns.* Second edition. Boston: Little, Brown and Company, 1969.

REDFORD, EMMETTE S., DAVID B. TRUMAN, ALAN F. WESTIN, and ROBERT C. WOOD. *Politics and Government in the United States.* Second edition. New York: Harcourt, Brace & World, Inc., 1968.

YOUNG, WILLIAM H. *Ogg & Ray's Essentials of American National Government.* Tenth edition. New York: Appleton-Century-Crofts, 1969.

KEY TO MAJOR TEXTBOOKS
(by chapters)

OUTLINE CHAPTERS	Adrian & Press	Burns & Peltason	Carr et al.	Cummings & Wise	Dahl	Diamond et al.	Ebenstein et al.	Ferguson & McHenry	Irish & Prothro	Nimmo & Ungs	Redford et al.	Young
1. The Fields of Political Science	1,2,3	1		1			1	3	1	1	1	1
2. The American Federal Union—Basic Features	4,5	2	2	1,2,3	8,9	2,3	4	4	2,3	3,4	2	
3. How It All Started—Birth of the United States	6	2	1,2,3	2	8,9	2,3	4	3,4	2,3	3,4	2,3	1
4. The Constitution of the United States	4,17	3,6,7	2,3	2	8,9	4,5	4,5	3,4	4,5	4	3	2
5. Federalism—An American Experiment	4,5,21	2,3,6,7	2,4,5	2,3	8,9	5	6	4,5	4	3	2,3	3
6. Evolving American Federalism	4,5,17	5	4,5	3	8,9		6	5	4			3
7. First Amendment Freedoms	4,18	6,7	19	1,4,5	4,6	14	9	6	13	3	14,17	4
8. Equality and Equal Protection	4,18	7	21	1,5	4,6,7	14	10	7	13	3	18	4
9. Citizenship, Rights, and Property	4,6,18	8	19	4	9		10	8	13	5	18	4
10. Public Opinion	6,11	9,10,11,12	10,11,14,17	6	19	13	11	9	5,7	6	4	6
11. Voting and the Voter	2,3,9,10,11,12	10,11	6,7,8,9,10	9	18,19,20	13	11	11	5,6,7	5,8,10	4,7	5,6
12. Interest Groups in Politics	7,10,11,17,19	11,12	7,9	6	20,21,22	10,11,12	11,12,14	9	6,7	5,6,7,8	4	6
13. Political Parties	6,8,9,10,11	12,13	6,7,9,10	7	18,20	10	12,13	10	6	5,7,9	5,6	7
14. Elections	10,11	12,13	9,10	8,9	22	12	11	11	8	8	7	8
15. The Organization of Congress	13,14	16,17	11,12	12	12,13,14	6	16	12	9	11	11,12	9
16. Congress at Work	13,14	16,17	13	12	14	6	16	13	9	11,13	11,12	10,11
17. The Presidency	15,16	14,15	14	10	10,11	7	17	14	10	12	9	11,12
18. The Presidential Establishment	15,16	15	15,16	10,11	10,11	7,8	18	15	10,11	14	10	13

KEY TO MAJOR TEXTBOOKS
(by chapters)

OUTLINE CHAPTERS	Adrian & Press	Burns & Peltason	Carr et al.	Cummings & Wise	Dahl	Diamond et al.	Ebenstein et al.	Ferguson & McHenry	Irish & Prothro	Nimmo & Ungs	Redford et al.	Young
19. Courts, Justice, and the Law	4,17,18	19	17,18	13	15,16,17	9	7,8	16	12	15	14,15,16	14
20. United States Foreign Policy	20	21	22	14		16	23	18	15		22	21
21. Conducting Foreign Relations	20	21,22,23	22	14		16	23	19	15		23	21
22. National Defense	20	22	22	14		16	23	20	14,15		23	22
23. The Growing Function of Regulation	16,19	24	23	11		8,15	20	21	14		19	15,16
24. What the Government Promotes	16,19	25	23,24	11,15		15	20,21	21,22	14		19,20,21	17,18,20
25. Managing Government Operations	16	26	16,23,24	15		15	19	17	11,14		19,24	19,23

Contents

CHAPTER 1

The Fields of Political Science

INTRODUCTION

In college course titles, the term, *political science,* is often used in a sense synonymous with the expression, *study of government.* Thus a course listed in one college catalog as Political Science 101 may be in most ways identical to a course listed in another college catalog as Government 101.

Political science is thus concerned with the study of formal government, as identified by such terms as *nation, state, city, school district,* etc. Political science is largely concerned with the power relationships which exist among these and other governmental units, and between the individual and each one of the governmental units.

But, while political science may be considered a specialized area of study itself, a number of specialized fields have developed within the area of political science. A detailed study of these would hold little interest for the student of a survey course in American national government, but a preliminary grasp of a few of the more basic fields will help him understand the large area to which he is directing his study.

I. SIX BASIC FIELDS OF POLITICAL SCIENCE

A. Political Theory

1. Concerned with basic premises concerning the nature of the state and man's role in it.
2. Includes the thinking and writing of such men as Plato, Aristotle, Hobbes, Locke, Montesquieu, Jefferson, Hamilton, Madison.

B. Public Law

1. Interested in constitutions, statutes, and other forms of the law.
2. Also concerned with institutions of government created by constitutions, their interrelationships, and the constitutional relationships among levels of government in one general system.
3. Judicial behavior is an important aspect, since constitutions and laws mean what the judges say they mean.

C. International Relations

1. Concerned with relationships between nations (states) in peace and war.
2. Has become increasingly interested in the study of international organizations and alliances among groups of nations.

D. Public Administration

1. Undertakes to study the structures of governmental organizations, the process of decision-making, and the *actual* location of power within the governmental bureaucracy.
2. Involves a search for structural defects within governmental organization and proposal of alternate structures and procedures.

E. Political Behavior

1. Interested in public opinion, its formation and measurement, and its effect on voting behavior.
2. Embraces the study of individual behavior and mass behavior in political processes, such as nominations and elections, motivations behind individual behavior.

F. Comparative

1. Undertakes to examine and compare related values, institutions, and governmental processes which have been adopted by different states.
2. Interested in the study of cultural, geographical, and other characteristics considered distinctive as bases for understanding differences in governments and political values.

Literally scores of specialization fields in political science could be added to this basic list. Indeed, these six basic fields could be further divided into an impressive list. On the other hand, it will be readily seen that the six fields of political science listed above overlap to a considerable degree.

II. RELATED SOCIAL SCIENCES

A. Economics

1. Interested in the study of production and wealth and its distribution, matters of increasing concern to all governments.
2. Shares with political science an interest in the role of the state in economic affairs, taxation, and regulation of commerce.

B. Geography

1. Embraces the study of man's relationship with his environment.
2. Closely related to political science, since political values and relationships are often influenced by characteristics of the natural environment.

C. History

1. Commonly constitutes the story of past politics.
2. Is important to political science in that history helps explain political institutions.

D. Psychology

1. The science of human behavior.
2. Helps in the analysis of political motivation, the nature of individual and mass opinion, and characteristics of political leadership.

E. Sociology

1. The parent science of society.
2. Provides political science with information concerning social institutions and social behavior.
3. Interested in the study of behavior common to members of groups of people.

III. SOME BASIC THEORIES OF GOVERNMENT AND THE STATE

A. Theory of Divine Right

1. The right of the ruler to rule was inherited from his ancestors, who were believed to have been appointed by a Supreme Being.
2. Identified with absolutist governments.

3. Was accepted as justification for the rule of kings in much of the Western world from the fifteenth through the eighteenth centuries.
4. This theory was weakened and replaced by the new contract theory, which held that a ruler's power was granted to him not by God, but by the sovereign people.

B. Economic Interest Theory

1. The primary role of government and of the state is to develop, promote, and protect economic interests such as trade, markets, commerce, and wealth.
2. Economic interests which thrive under protection of the state are powerful in determining the direction of governmental policy.

C. Force Theory

1. Holds that the state is a product of force and conquest.
2. Like other theories, it cannot be proved, and is generally considered inadequate as an explanation of the origin of the state.

D. Kinship Theory

1. The state is merely an extension of the idea of the family.
2. The ruler is accepted as an analogy with the father as head of the family.

E. Contract Theory

1. Based on a basic agreement that man emerged from a state of nature and that necessity or conveniences caused men to form the basic institutions of government.
2. Contract theories have been advanced by several political thinkers, like John Locke, Jean Jacques Rousseau, and James Harrington. All, in one way or another, propose that the source of the power of government is the individual who is governed.
3. The American Declaration of Independence is largely based on the *contract theory of John Locke*, which is distinctive for its proposal that when the ruler ceased to act in the interest of the governed, then the people have a right to withdraw from the ruler the power they have granted him to govern.
4. Great ideas fostered by the contract theory remain a part of the democratic concept, although the theory itself has faded from vogue.

IV. CLASSIFICATIONS OF GOVERNMENT

Governments have been classified in many different ways, according to specific characteristics and interests. The following five classifications are perhaps best known.

A. It is Generally Acknowledged That the State Has at Least These Five Essential Characteristics:

1. Population.
   a. No specific size of population is required.
   b. It is, however, generally agreed that an unoccupied territory or an uninhabited island cannot constitute a state.
2. Territory.
   a. May vary from less than one square mile to millions of square miles.
   b. Lacking a fixed territory, nomadic bands are not commonly thought of as states.
3. Permanence.
   a. Even Rome succumbed to the ravages of time.
   b. Relative degree of permanence, however, is necessary.

4. Government or political organization.
   a. State does not cease to exist when the form of government changes.
   b. Government may be of any ideological form.
5. Sovereignty.
   a. Absolute sovereignty may not exist.
   b. State must have relatively complete independence from external pressures.
   c. Lack of sovereignty is the major feature which keeps numerous governmental agencies, such as school boards, from identity as states.

B. Classification of States by Number and Quality of Rulers

This was a favorite method of classification among the early Greek philosophers. The following classification by Aristotle is perhaps best known:

GOVERNMENT BY	IN THE INTEREST OF ALL	IN THE RULERS' INTEREST
One	Monarchy	Tyranny
A few	Aristocracy	Oligarchy
Many	Polity	Democracy

C. Classification of States by the Relationship Between the Executive and the Legislature

1. Presidential government.
   a. Distinctive feature is that the executive is elected independently of the legislature and holds office for a fixed period. Also has extensive power not subject to control by the legislature.
   b. The term, *presidential government*, is descriptive of the system employed by the United States.
2. Cabinet or parliamentary government.
   a. Policy-making executives are the Prime Minister and his Cabinet, all of whom are members of the legislature and dependent on support of the legislature for continuance in office.
   b. Differs from the American system of *separation of powers* in that executive authority is dependent on the legislature.
   c. Principal advantage over presidential system is that when control of the legislative branch passes from one party to another, control of the executive branch passes with it. Thus it leaves no room for the "tug-of-war" which often exists between the American President of one party, when Congress is controlled by the other party.

D. Classification According to the Location of Power in Government

1. Confederation.
   a. Loose union of states in which the principal powers of government (perhaps *all* the real power) are retained by the individual member states.
   b. Central government exists to perform a limited number of functions, such as national defense.
   c. The United States was a confederation for eight years under the Articles of Confederation.
   d. There are many historical examples, but no *true* confederation exists today.
2. Federation.
   a. *Defined:* A federation, such as the United States, is a union of two or more local governments under one central government, *with both the central and the local governments exercising independent spheres of authority, either in theory or in practice.*
   b. Encourages unity in matters of general concern, but autonomy (independent authority) in matters of local concern.

c. Was originated by authors of the United States Constitution, following eight years of experimentation under the Articles of Confederation.
3. Unitary government.
    a. One in which the whole power of government is vested in one central government, from which local governments derive their authority.
    b. England and France are examples.
    c. Unitary government is not incompatible with democracy.

E. Classification of States by the Degree of Governmental Regulation of the Lives of Individuals

1. Anarchism.
    a. Holds that all government is evil, unnecessary, and undesirable.
    b. Man is naturally cooperative. Left to himself, he will spontaneously enter into cooperation with his fellow men whenever group action is necessary.
    c. Man reaches his highest development when unrestrained by government, which always represents repressive force.
    d. Many anarchists have viewed the state as an instrument of the upper classes, a tool for their use in exploiting the lower classes.
2. Individualism.
    a. Advocates the restriction of governmental activities within narrow limits, leaving a broad area of freedom to the individual.
    b. Concedes that government is necessary, but is a necessary evil which must be narrowly restricted.
    c. Extreme view is that government should confine its activities to the protection of private property, should not regulate business, and should not enter into business.
    d. In the economic world, embraces the *laissez-faire* philosophy, holding that if the individual is left unregulated, self-interest will cause him to act in the interest of society.
3. Socialism.
    a. Stands for relatively rapid and sweeping economic collectivism (government ownership).
    b. Is sometimes defined as a state or society in which the principal means of producing and distributing wealth are collectively owned and operated (by the government).
    c. Content to rely on constitutional means to bring about the system, whereas Communists would carry the system much further and would resort to revolution.

F. Classification According to Limitation on Governmental Power

1. Dictatorship.
    a. Government resting on the will of a single person or a small group of persons.
    b. Have existed throughout recorded history.
    c. Often use sham legislatures to give appearance of popular support.
    d. Fearing hostile public opinion, dictators maintain tight control of the press.
    e. Welfare of state often held above welfare of individual.
    f. Examples are communism, which stresses class conflict and a collective economy, and fascism, which emphasizes race and national strength.
2. Democracy.
    a. Primary meaning is **government by the people.**
    b. **Indirect** democracy implies government by the people's representatives, as in the United States.
    c. Has always implied a government in which the people — or a majority of them — may act from time to time to elect or replace the policy-makers.
    d. Places high value on the individual and seeks to safeguard basic individual freedoms.

IDEOLOGICAL TERMINOLOGY

In everyday streetcorner conversation a number of terms are used commonly—perhaps too commonly—to reflect political values, that is to say, basic political ideologies. Thus one may hear Senator Barry Goldwater, or another of his political prominence, referred to as a "reactionary." The late President John F. Kennedy may similarly be referred to as a "liberal," or Senator Strom Thurmond of South Carolina as a "conservative."

All of these are peculiarly mercurial terms. What are the political values and beliefs of one who may accurately be described as *liberal* or *conservative* or *radical* or *reactionary?*

One of the most difficult jobs of the political scientist is to generalize in a situation where no generalization can be made with total accuracy. And in the realm of terminology, he meets perhaps the greatest difficulty of generalization—value terminology, that is. Value words such as those mentioned above cannot be precisely defined to the satisfaction of all onlookers. But this doesn't mean that the student must throw up his hands in despair and beat a hasty retreat from the subject.

Although these value terms, to repeat, *cannot* be concisely defined to the satisfaction of all persons, they can nonetheless be discussed, thought about, reflected on. In this manner, it is hoped, each individual may arrive at his own enlightened understanding of the terms, and if the discussion has been effective, one might hope to find important similarities at the base of individual understandings of the troublesome value words. If this is true, then the political discussion may proceed with a reasonable hope for effective communication and mutual understanding.

In the realm of political values, the terms, *liberal* and *conservative* are perhaps the most difficult. And yet, through the years, enough definite characteristics have attached to the two concepts to suggest a fairly stable diagram of a number of the conflicts between liberal and conservative values. The following list of conflicting characteristics common to liberalism and conservatism, respectively, may help lead to an understanding of their general political natures:

LIBERALISM EMBRACES	CONSERVATISM EMBRACES
Civil rights	Property rights
Welfare state	Individualism
Large government	Small government
Centralism	States' rights
Positive government	Government as referee
Internationalism	Nationalism, patriotism
Skepticism	Formal religion
Experimentation	Tradition (status quo)

It is probably fair to describe liberalism and conservatism as *establishmentarian* political values or creeds, since liberals and conservatives find no difficulty in operating side by side within the traditional established political context. Compromise is the assumed avenue to accord.

Compromise is perhaps less acceptable to *radicals* and *reactionaries.* To a large degree, these terms are labels of contempt, and thus have no real meaning in the context of political science. But to leave it at that would certainly be to capitulate.

It is often said that the terms *radical* and *reactionary* represent extremist political values which cannot operate or maneuver effectively within the established political structures. This is no doubt at least partially true. But it must be noted that this paradefinition leaves Senator Barry Goldwater out of the ranks of reactionaries, since he offered himself as a candidate for President.

If it is agreed that *radical* and *reactionary* are terms reflecting political extremism, then it must be said further that *reaction* is extremism of the right wing, that is to say, ultra-conservatism. It is often said that the reactionary wants to go back to the values of past generations (Men were men in those days!). **Radical** is often used to describe extremism of the left wing, impatience with evolutionary change, a willingness to resort to violence to bring about change. However, *radical* can be, and often is, used to describe extremism in any form. Thus it may be accurately said that reactionaries are right-wing radicals.

SELECTED TEST QUESTIONS

I. Multiple Choice

1. Civil rights and the welfare state are often said to be values embraced by the:
   (a) liberal; (b) conservative; (c) radical; (d) reactionary.
2. Patriotism and tradition are often said to be values embraced by:
   (a) liberalism; (b) conservatism; (c) radicalism; (d) reaction.
3. The field of political science interested in public opinion and elections is called:
   (a) political theory; (b) public law; (c) comparative; (d) political behavior.
4. The source of governmental power is the individual, says the:
   (a) divine right theory; (b) force theory; (c) kinship theory; (d) contract theory.
5. John Locke is identified with the:
   (a) contract theory; (b) economic interest theory; (c) divine right theory; (d) kinship theory.

II. True-False

1. According to Aristotle, government by many in the rulers' interest is democracy.
2. The unitary system of government typifies a dictatorship.
3. Federalism typifies a democratic system of government.
4. A characteristic of confederation is an equal division of powers between two levels of government.
5. The United States typifies the presidential form of government.

CHAPTER 2

The American Federal Union–
Basic Features

INTRODUCTION

An understanding of a system of government might best be approached by examining its unique features—that is to say, by studying what makes it distinct and different from other governments. It is said that the United States is a democracy. It is said that England is a democracy. Does this mean that England and the United States have identical systems of government? Not by any means.

It is true that the governments of both the United States and England are characterized by democratic values. That is to say, the people of both the United States and England have opportunity through the established channels of government and custom to influence the determination of public policy and the selection of national leaders. There, it would seem, the structural similarities between the two governments end.

It might seem that the best approach to a study of the government of the United States would begin with an examination of five basic features of the national government: the *separation of powers* principle, *federalism*, the *presidency, judicial review*, and *representative democracy*.

I. SEPARATION OF POWERS

A. Sometimes Referred to as "Checks and Balances"

B. Undertook a Permanent Division of Governmental Authority Among the Executive (Presidential), Legislative (Congress), and Judicial (Courts), Branches of Government in Such a Way That Each Could act Independently of the Other Two, but Would Still Have a Check to Prevent the Other Two from Exceeding the Legal Limits of Their Power. Examples:

1. President may veto acts of Congress.
2. Congress may override presidential veto by two-thirds majority vote in both houses.
3. Courts may declare acts of either President or Congress unconstitutional, thus void.

C. Officials of Each of Three Branches Selected by Different Procedures

1. President elected indirectly by nationwide vote for four-year term and may be reelected only once.
2. Judges appointed by President, with Senate approval, to serve for life and may be removed only by impeachment or death.

D. Separation Not Complete Insofar as Officials of Each Branch Participate in Affairs of Other Two

1. Acts of Congress require signature of President before becoming law.
2. Court orders sometimes require enforcement by President.
3. Treaties negotiated by executive department require approval by Senate.
4. Legislation recommended by President requires approval by both houses of Congress.
5. Congress dependent on President for legislative leadership.
6. President dependent on Congress for legislative enactment of his proposals.

8

E. Serves to Insure That the Same Person or Group Will Not Make the Law, Enforce the Law, and Interpret the Law

1. Legislature (Congress) makes the law.
2. President sees that the law is enforced.
3. Courts interpret and apply the law.

F. Advantages of Separation-of-Powers Principle

1. Prevents usurpation of power by any one agency of government.
2. Prevents arbitrary treatment of the individual, which might result if all powers were centered in one agency of government.
3. Encourages broad deliberation before government acts.

G. Disadvantages of Separation-of-Powers Principle

1. Creates complexity in government which makes it difficult for the individual to understand governmental processes.
2. Creates delay, since it is designed to stifle expeditious action.
3. Causes conflicts between the three branches of government.

H. Separation-of-Powers Principle Was Advocated by Montesquieu, the French Writer in His 1748 book, *Spirit of the Laws*

I. All 50 States of the American Union Have Adopted the Principle in Their Constitutions

II. FEDERALISM

A. Basically Involves a Division of Governmental Power (Sovereignty) Between Two (or More) Levels of Government, Such as the National and State Governments in the United States (See Chapter 5)

1. Was thought impossible prior to the American experiment.
2. Men who wrote U.S. Constitution "invented" federalism.
3. Natural outgrowth of problems experienced under Articles of Confederation.

B. In the American System It Means That the States Are Sovereign in Matters of Local Concern, While the National Government Is Sovereign in Matters of General (Nationwide) Concern

III. THE PRESIDENCY

A. A Unique Office in the Method by Which It Is Filled, Its Relationship with the Legislative Branch, and the Powers Which May Be Exercised (See Chapter 17)

B. President Elected by Indirect Popular Vote Every Four Years

C. Most Powerful Public Office in the World

D. Only Office in the American Government Intended to be Responsive to the Will of *All* the People

E. Because of the Separation-of-Powers Principle, the Office Is Vested with Numerous Powers Relatively Free of Control by Congress

F. Office Has Shown Steady Growth in Power Throughout Its History

IV. JUDICIAL REVIEW

A. Refers to the Power of Federal Courts, and Especially the Supreme Court, to Interpret the Constitution and to Declare Acts of Congress or the President Void as Conflicting with the Constitution (See Chapter 19)

   1. A power not written into the Constitution, but seized upon by the Supreme Court under Chief Justice John Marshall in the 1803 case of *Marbury v. Madison.*
   2. Invalidation of a congressional act may be overcome only by "corrective" legislation by Congress or by a constitutional amendment.

B. Judicial Review of the Acts of State Legislature Is a Practice of the Courts in Each of the American States

V. REPRESENTATIVE DEMOCRACY

A. Differs from "Direct" Democracy in That Government Is Conducted Not by the People Themselves, but by Their Elected Representatives

B. Only Kind of Democracy in Existence Today

C. Was Considered "Radical" Idea When United States Was Founded

D. Was Break with Past in Basic Assumptions

   1. Primary role of government is to enable each person to achieve his highest potential of development.
   2. Individual liberty—greatest amount of individual freedom consistent with order.
   3. Political equality.
   4. Fraternity—an assumption that all men will use their freedom from governmental control in such a way as to promote the welfare of society in general.
   5. Popular sovereignty—ultimate political power resting with the people.
   6. Majority control over public policy, but protection of fundamental rights of all in such matters as speech, press, religion, assembly, petition, and equality before the law.

E. Often Considered Synonymous with *Republican* Form of Government

VI. BASIC THEORY OF AMERICAN DEMOCRACY: LIMITED POWER

A. Three Separations of Power

   1. Functional separation.
      a. Legislative.
      b. Executive.
      c. Judicial.
   3. Geographical separation.
      a. Power of national government.
      b. Power of state governments.
   3. Separation of power over time.
      a. Federal judges appointed for life.
      b. Precedent serves as restraint on future generations.

B. Other Limits on Official Power

1. Constitutional restraints.
2. Judicial restraints.
3. Custom.
4. Public opinion.
5. Political-party vigilance.

SELECTED TEST QUESTIONS

I. Multiple Choice

1. The separation-of-powers principle in the United States was advocated by:
   (a) Rousseau; (b) Locke; (c) Socrates; (d) Montesquieu.
2. Division of sovereignty between two levels of government is typical of:
   (a) federalism; (b) confederation; (c) unitary government; (d) democracy.
3. The Supreme Court seized for itself the power of judicial review in the case of:
   (a) *McCulloch v. Maryland;* (b) *Marbury v. Madison;* (c) *Barron v. Baltimore;* (d) *Plessy v. Ferguson.*
4. A term often used properly as synonymous with *representative democracy* is:
   (a) oligarchy; (b) aristocracy; (c) republican government; (d) dictatorship.
5. Fraternity and individual liberty are characteristics of:
   (a) unitary government; (b) federalism; (c) confederation; (d) democracy.

II. True-False

1. The term "checks and balances" refers to the division of governmental power between the national government and the state governments.
2. Governmental power was dispersed in the American system as a protection against excessively centralized authority.
3. The men who wrote the United States Constitution were primarily interested in creating an efficient form of government.
4. The Cabinet form of government reasonably assures political identity between the legislative and executive branches.
5. The American principle of separation of powers was borrowed from the English system of government.

CHAPTER 3

How It All Started–
Birth of the United States

INTRODUCTION

Political historians often divide the political history of the United States into three distinct periods: (1) the 168 years from the founding of the first permanment English settlement at Jamestown in 1607 until the Declaration of Independence in 1775; (2) the 14 years beginning with the Declaration of Independence and ending with the launching of our present government under the Constitution of 1787; and (3) the American experience since 1789 under what is now the oldest written constitution in existence.

I. COLONIAL BACKGROUND

A. Government of Thirteen Colonies Based upon Thirteen Separate Written Charters of Three Types

1. Royal colonies.
    a. Included the seven colonies of Georgia, New Hampshire, New Jersey, New York, North Carolina, South Carolina, and Virginia. Massachusetts, too, became a royal colony in 1691.
    b. Were governed directly by the king after their charters were revoked.
2. Proprietary colonies.
    a. Included Delaware, Maryland, and Pennsylvania.
    b. Were owned and ruled by the proprietor.
3. Charter colonies.
    a. Included Connecticut, Massachusetts (before 1691), and Rhode Island.
    b. Had greatest measure of independence, with colonial governors elected by their own legislatures.

B. Features of the Colonial Governments

1. Authority divided among legislative, executive, and judicial branches.
2. Two-house (bicameral) legislature in each colony except Pennsylvania.
    a. Members of each upper house appointed.
    b. Members of each lower house elected.
3. Governors of royal and proprietary colonies were powerful, having the power of absolute veto of legislature and command of colonial militia.
4. Only elected assemblies could levy taxes or appropriate money to be spent.

II. GROWING COLONIAL AFFILIATION

A. Colonists Familiar with Handling Domestic Problems of Government, but Inexperienced in Dealing with Intercolonial Affairs

B. **Events Leading to Intercolonial Affiliation**

  1. *New England Confederation.*
     a. Organized in 1643 to consider threats to colonial security posed by Indians, Dutch, and French.
     b. Effective organization until 1664.
  2. *The Albany Plan.*
     a. Grew out of a conference called by the British in 1754 of representatives of the seven northern colonies to discuss Indian affairs.
     b. Benjamin Franklin grasped the occasion to propose his plan for continental government (the Albany Plan).
     c. Called for a Grand Council composed of representatives elected by the colonial assemblies and a presiding officer to be appointed by the king. Council would regulate trade with Indians, determine war and peace, levy taxes, and provide for needed military and naval forces.
  3. *French and Indian War (Seven Years' War, 1756-63).*
     a. Inspired spirit of unity and identity among colonists.
     b. Produced first "American" war heroes.
     c. Culmination of warfare between the British and the French in North America from 1689 until 1763.
     d. Ended in British victory over France in struggle for control of North America.
     e. British victory followed by increased attention toward the colonies and plans to tax the colonists to help pay for colonial defense.
  4. The *Stamp Act Congress* met in New York in October, 1765, and declared that the new stamp taxes levied on the colonists by the Crown could not be collected without the people's consent.
  5. *Committees of Correspondence* — began organizing in 1772 to secretly spread word throughout the colonies of latest acts by the Crown.

III. THE CONTINENTAL CONGRESSES

A. **First Continental Congress Met in Philadelphia in 1774**

  1. Petitioned the British king and Parliament to repeal taxation and other measures considered oppressive by the colonists.
  2. Declared the rights of colonists to make own laws, except in area of foreign trade.

B. **Second Continental Congress Met in Philadelphia in 1775**

  1. Assumed duties of a limited government, uniting the colonies for the war effort.
  2. Organized an army and appointed George Washington Commander in Chief.
  3. Caused to be written, and then approved, the *Declaration of Independence.*
  4. Encouraged the colonies to set themselves up as states.
  5. Had no *legal* authority, but was the only agency unifying the newly independent states until March 1, 1781, when it was succeeded by the Congress of the Confederation, formed under the Articles of Confederation.

IV. THE DECLARATION OF INDEPENDENCE

A. **Written by Thomas Jefferson for the Second Continental Congress in 1776**

B. **Based on the Reasoning and Prose of John Locke in His *Second Treatise of Civil Government*, Which Locke Wrote in 1689 as a Philosophical Justification for the English Bloodless Revolution of 1688**

C. Views Government as a *Social Contract* and Stresses the *Natural Rights of Man*

V. THE ARTICLES OF CONFEDERATION

A. Grew Out of a Resolution Adopted by the Second Continental Congress in July, 1776, for Formation of "a League of Friendship"

B. Took Effect in 1781, When Maryland Became the Thirteenth State to Ratify

C. Major Provisions
1. Continued sovereignty of the states.
2. Created one central agency—the unicameral Congress of the Confederation, in which each member state would have an equal vote.
3. Did not create a *national government,* because the Congress of the Confederation was vested with no sovereign powers.
4. Delegates to be chosen by the state legislatures and their salaries paid by the states.
5. No power to tax or to regulate commerce vested in the new Congress.
6. No executive or judicial branch was created for the new government.
7. In Congress, approval of nine of the thirteen states was required on important decisions.
8. Amendments to the Articles required ratification by all thirteen states.
9. Congress was empowered to determine peace and war, make treaties, coin money, regulate trade with the Indians, issue bills of credit, build and equip a navy, establish a postal system, and to appoint senior officers in the state militias.
10. Lacking the power to tax, Congress was dependent on the states to contribute to the cost of the central government in response to requisitions, which the states were inclined to ignore or discount.

VI. DISILLUSIONMENT AND THE MOVE FOR REVISION

A. Problems Under Confederation
1. Trade problems.
   a. Loss of trading privileges which had been enjoyed as colonies of the British Empire.
   b. Difficulty of negotiating acceptable commercial treaties with other nations growing out of European belief that treaties would not be honored.
   c. Mississippi River closed at New Orleans to American goods.
   d. American ships victimized by Barbary pirates in Mediterranean.
   e. Interference with business and commerce by the states.
2. Monetary problems.
   a. No uniform and stable medium of exchange.
   b. Money coined by each of the states.
   c. Money issued by Congress virtually worthless.
   d. Both Congress and states unable to pay war debts and meet other obligations.
   e. Legislative tampering with obligations of debtors.
3. Structural weaknesses of the Articles.
   a. Dependency of Congress on state legislatures.
      (1) Inability of Congress to compel state legislatures to contribute money toward the support of the war effort and the maintenance of the central government.
      (2) Inability of Congress to compel state legislatures to honor requisitions for troops needed to prosecute the war.

      (3) Inability of Congress to compel the states to protect property rights and enforce the obligations of contracts.

   b. Financial instability resulting from lack of power to tax.

   c. Instability of domestic direction growing out of lack of executive officer.

   d. Instability of international direction resulting from lack of exclusive authority in international relations.

   e. Instability of legal/judicial administration arising from the fact of thirteen separate legal/judicial systems and no standardization of legal/judicial processes.

   f. Instability of conditions of interstate trade brought about by inability of Congress to establish uniform trade regulations.

B. Pressures for Strengthening the Articles

1. Alexander Hamilton had considered them unworkably weak from the beginning.
   a. As Washington's aide during the war, he became disgusted with failure of the states to support the war effort.
   b. Consistently favored strong central government.
2. *Annapolis Convention.*
   a. Meeting called by Virginia legislature in 1786 to offer all states opportunity to resolve trade rivalries.
   b. Nine states appointed delegates, but representatives from only five actually showed up.
   c. Delegates present petitioned Congress to summon a convention of representatives from all states to consider possible methods of strengthening the central government and making it more effective.
   d. Congress responded by summoning such a convention to meet in Philadelphia in May, 1787, for the sole purpose of revising the Articles of Confederation to make them "adequate to the exigencies of government and the preservation of the Union."
3. *Shays's Rebellion.*
   a. Promoted the cause of a stronger union by justifying declarations that the dangers of dissolution and anarchy were real and immediate.
   b. In winter of 1786-87, grew out of refusal by Massachusetts legislature to provide relief for farmers facing imprisonment for inability to meet mortgage payments and pay taxes.
   c. Was led by Daniel Shays, Revolutionary War captain under Washington.
   d. Was quickly suppressed by militia, after farmers had forcibly prevented foreclosure of mortgages on their farms at the courthouse in Northampton, Massachusetts.
4. Interests and the proposal for revision.
   a. Favoring revision.
      (1) Property interests.
      (2) Shipping interests.
      (3) Businessmen.
   b. Opposing revision.
      (1) Farmers.
      (2) Debtors.
      (3) "State Nationalists."

VII. THE CONSTITUTIONAL CONVENTION

A. The Delegates

1. Represented every state except Rhode Island.

2. Seventy-four delegates were named by the states to attend.
3. Fifty-five actually attended at one time or another.
4. About forty took part in the convention.
5. Included many of the most important men of the nation—men of property and substance, merchants, planters, bankers, political leaders.
6. Basically a conservative assemblage, only eight of the signers of the Declaration of Independence were included.

B. The Leaders

1. *George Washington.*
   a. Presided.
   b. Prestige lent much dignity to the convention.
2. *James Madison.*
   a. Like Washington, a delegate from Virginia.
   b. At thirty-six, he was perhaps best prepared of the delegates, having made extensive constitutional studies.
   c. Kept most complete record of proceedings.
3. *Alexander Hamilton.*
   a. Had long advocated a strong central government.
   b. Served as aide to Washington in the war.
4. *Benjamin Franklin*, Pennsylvania delegate of broad reputation.
5. *Gouverneur Morris*, Pennsylvania delegate and aristocrat.

C. Convention Highlights

1. Congress had authorized the convention to suggest amendments to the Articles of Confederation, but this goal was promptly discarded as the delegates elected to propose instead a more powerful central government with powers of its own.
2. Sessions met behind closed doors in Independence Hall, meeting place of the Pennsylvania legislature.
3. Provision for a national executive and independent judiciary won ready agreement.
4. Deadlock over congressional representation.
   a. Franklin preferred a one-house (unicameral) national legislature, but most delegates, accustomed to bicameralism in state legislatures, wanted two houses.
   b. Representation based on population favored by large states like Virginia, Massachusetts, and Pennsylvania.
   c. Equal representation for states, as provided in the Articles of Confederation, favored by small states like New Jersey.
   d. Issue caused severe deadlock.
   e. Solution through the *Connecticut Compromise* called for a two-house legislature.
      (1) Lower house with representation based on population, in which all revenue and appropriation measures would originate.
      (2) Upper house with equal representation for each state.
5. Two prefabricated plans for revision.
   a. *Virginia Plan.*
      (1) Submitted to the Convention by Edmund Randolph, Virginia delegate.
      (2) Would have scrapped the Articles of Confederation in favor of a new and strong national government.
      (3) Called for a national executive and judiciary.

(4) Prescribed a two-house legislature with representation based on population or wealth.

(5) Congress would hold veto over state legislation.

(6) Congress would have broad powers over matters of national concern.

(7) Was main topic of discussion during opening days of convention.

(8) Had strong support from larger states.

  b. *New Jersey Plan.*

(1) Submitted to the Convention by William Paterson, New Jersey delegate.

(2) Represented views of small states and states' rights advocates.

(3) Designed as counterproposal to the Virginia Plan.

(4) Provided one-house legislature.

(5) Equal vote for each state.

(6) Was aimed at moderate modification of Articles of Confederation.

6. Provisions for ratification and amendment.

  a. Articles of Confederation had required ratification by all thirteen states before they became effective and ratification by all the states before amendments could be adopted.

  b. New Constitution was to become effective when ratified by nine states, and approval of three-fourths of states would be required for amendments.

  c. New Constitution was to go into effect when approved by *popularly elected conventions,* rather than the legislatures, of nine states—a provision intended to circumvent expected hostility in state legislatures and give the Constitution highest legal status.

VIII. PUBLIC REACTION AND DRIVE FOR RATIFICATION

A. Popular Response

1. Praise for new document voiced in Europe.

2. Sharp division of attitudes voiced in states.

  a. Arguments in support of ratification.

(1) Alternative was weakness, indecision, and anarchy.

(2) Confederation had been too weak to effectively support the war and was too weak to solve problems of the postwar period.

(3) Liberty depended on union, and union on the stability offered by the new Constitution.

(4) The Constitution embraced the true principles of republican government.

(5) The Constitution wasn't perfect, but improvements could be made as deficiencies appeared.

  b. Arguments against ratification.

(1) Included no bill of rights.

(2) Was written by aristocrats to support their interests.

(3) Such a concentration of power would imperil republican principles and individual liberty.

(4) Would threaten independence of the states.

3. Emerging political-party alignments.

  a. *Federalists* was the name adopted by like-minded political leaders and followers who advocated ratification and the resulting stronger central government.

  b. *Antifederalists* was the name applied to those who either opposed ratification of the new Constitution, or opposed the precipitate haste with which Federalists were urging ratification.

4. The War of Words.

  a. *The Federalist* is the name assigned to a series of newspaper articles written and published in support of the drive for ratification of the new Constitution. Written with much dignity and fairness, *The Federalist Papers,* as they were first known, consist of 85 essays undertaking

to explain provisions of the new Constitution. They were written for a New York newspaper by Alexander Hamilton, James Madison, and John Jay.
  b. *Letters of the Federal Farmer* is the name given to a series of essays written by Richard Henry Lee of Virginia urging deliberation instead of haste in the ratification drive and pointing out flaws in the proposed constitution.
 5. Ratification by states.
  a. Much apathy remained on the part of the general public, which nonetheless elected the ratifying conventions.
  b. Order of ratification by states.
   (1) Delaware, December 7, 1787, by unanimous vote in convention.
   (2) Pennsylvania, December 15, 1787, by 46-23 vote in convention.
   (3) New Jersey, December 18, 1787, by unanimous vote in convention.
   (4) Georgia, January 2, 1788, by unanimous vote in convention.
   (5) Connecticut, January 4, 1788, by 128-42 vote in convention.
   (6) Massachusetts, February 6, 1788, by 187-168 vote in convention.
   (7) Maryland, April 26, 1788, by 63-11 vote in convention.
   (8) South Carolina, May 23, 1788, by 149-73 vote in convention.
   (9) New Hampshire, June 21, 1788, by 57-47 vote in convention.
   (10) Virginia, June 25, 1788, by 89-79 vote in convention.
   (11) New York, July 26, 1788, by 30-27 vote in convention.
   (12) North Carolina, November 21, 1789, by 194-77 vote in convention.
   (13) Rhode Island, May 28, 1790, by 34-32 vote in convention.

SELECTED TEST QUESTIONS

I. Multiple Choice

1. The Articles of Confederation can best be described as:
(a) a tight, binding charter for national government; (b) a charter for a league of friendship; (c) a charter which centralized governmental power; (d) a charter which divided sovereignty about equally between two levels of government.
2. Although Thomas Jefferson is commonly acknowledged as author of the Declaration of Independence, the reasoning is that of:
(a) Locke; (b) Montesquieu; (c) Rousseau; (d) Hamilton.
3. Under the Articles of Confederation, the central government was financed by:
(a) a tax on property; (b) a tax on incomes; (c) a tax on commerce; (d) contributions from the states.
4. In the bicameral colonial legislatures, members of the upper houses commonly achieved office by:
(a) popular election; (b) inheritance; (c) competitive examination; (d) appointment.
5. One of the major criticisms of the new Constitution was that it:
(a) was too democratic; (b) provided no president for the nation; (c) contained no bill of rights; (d) was too weak.

II. True-False

1. Some, but not all, of the American colonies had bicameral legislatures.
2. Benjamin Franklin's Albany Plan called for political independence of the colonies.
3. The First Continental Congress petitioned the British king for tax revision.
4. The Articles of Confederation created a single, central governmental agency—a unicameral legislative body.
5. John Locke believed that men had certain *natural rights*.

CHAPTER 4

The Constitution of the United States

INTRODUCTION

Working behind closed doors during the hot summer of 1787, a group of distinguished representatives from twelve of the American states debated, contended, espoused, and compromised until they had produced a proposed new Constitution of the United States of America. When the doors were thrown open and the results of their handiwork revealed to the world, a mixed response followed.

Although the new document was instantly hailed by some scholars in Europe, it nonetheless was viewed with suspicion and misgiving by many in the states who were expected to play a role in its adoption as the basic law of the land.

The agrarian and debtor classes had not wanted it in the first place and were disinclined to be pleased. They were satisfied with the simpler and weaker Articles of Confederation. They had had no representatives at the convention, and some viewed the entire affair as a conspiracy promoted by the "better" members of the community. Much of their suspicion was based on the fact that the new Constitution included no Bill of Rights with assurances of individual liberty—such as were common in the state constitutions. They drew little comfort from assurances by Hamilton and others that a Bill of Rights would be unnecessary, and that Article I did impose restraints on powers of the states and on the proposed new national government.

I. THE CONSTITUTION AS A RESTRAINT ON GOVERNMENTAL POWER

A. National Power—the Separation Principle

1. Powers carefully separated and balanced among executive, legislative, and judicial branches.
2. Purpose was to avoid centralization of powers and resultant tyranny.
3. Undertook to divide governmental powers so each of three departments would be jealous of encroachments.
4. Careful balance of dependency, independence, and interdependency established among three departments.
5. Judicial branch often said to be most independent of three, but federal judges may be impeached and removed from office by Congress.
6. Presidential veto is outstanding example of executive check on legislative branch.
7. Control of purse strings is outstanding example of legislative check on executive branch.
8. Power to interpret Constitution and laws is outstanding example of check judiciary holds over President and Congress.
9. Power of enforcement of court decisions is major check of executive over judicial branch.
10. Principle was not aimed at achieving efficiency in government, but security from tyranny.
11. Historical developments affecting the separation.
    a. Development of political parties.
       (1) Has provided basis for cooperation between President and Congress.
       (2) Checks and balances system has weakened the parties.
    b. Electoral changes.
       (1) President's selection is more nearly expression of popular will than was intended.

(2) Prior to adoption of the seventeenth amendment in 1913, U.S. Senators were elected by state legislature; since then, they have been popularly elected.

(3) Ratification of the Bill of Rights in 1791 placed restraints on all departments of national government and served to give the courts additional checks on executive and legislative branches.

(4) Executive power has experienced steady growth, while congressional power, by relationship, has ebbed in the twentieth century.

(5) Creation of regulatory agencies (such as the Interstate Commerce Commission), beginning late in the nineteenth century, has had tendency to combine executive, legislative, and judicial functions in the making of detailed, routine economic decisions.

(6) Twenty-second amendment (1951) limits President to two elected terms.

B. Restraints on State Power

1. Article I, Section 10.
   a. Forbids states to enter treaties, license piracy, coin money, subvert the national currency, pass "any bill of attainder, *ex post facto* law, or law impairing the obligation of contracts, or grant any title of nobility."
   b. Outlaws tariffs by states.
   c. Forbids states to maintain armies and navies, or engage in war (but see Amendment II).
2. Supremacy of Constitution, laws, and treaties of the United States (see Article VI).
3. Fourteenth amendment.
   a. Defines citizenship, providing supremacy of national citizenship over state citizenship.
   b. Restrains states from—
      (1) Abridging privileges and immunities of United States citizens.
      (2) Depriving persons of life, liberty, or property without due process of law.
      (3) Denying persons equal protection of the laws.
4. Fifteenth amendment.
   a. Third of the three Civil War amendments (thirteenth, fourteenth, and fifteenth).
   b. Intended to guarantee Negroes' right to vote.
5. Nineteenth amendment.
   a. Forbids states to deny women right to vote.
   b. Adopted in 1920
6. Twenty-fourth amendment.
   a. Proposed in 1962 and adopted in 1964.
   b. Forbids states to collect poll tax as prerequisite to voting in election for President or Congress.
   c. Poll tax remained legal as prerequisite for voting for local and state officers.

II. THE CONSTITUTION AS A FRAMEWORK FOR NATIONAL GOVERNMENT

A. Article I

1. Creates a bicameral national legislature with delegated powers, some of them exclusive, and *all* the lawmaking authority of the new government.
2. Creates qualifications for membership in the national legislature.
3. Places restraints on state legislatures.

B. Article II

1. Creates a national executive.
2. Briefly defines the role, responsibility, and powers of the President.
3. Establishes qualifications for the office of President.

C. Article III

1. Provides for creation of a Supreme Court.
2. Authorizes Congress to establish inferior courts.
3. Provides life tenure for judges of "both the supreme and inferior courts."
4. Establishes jurisdiction of national courts.
5. Guarantees jury trial.
6. Defines treason.

D. Article IV

1. Full-Faith-and-Credit Clause—Provides that judicial proceedings of any state shall be honored by all other states.
2. Privileges-and-Immunities Clause—"The citizens of each State shall be entitled to all privileges and immunities of citizens in the several States." (But no effort is made to define citizenship.)
3. Extradition Clause—Provides for the forcible return of fugitives from one state to another. (However, this provision has been made discretionary by decision of the U.S. Supreme Court.)
4. States' Admission Clause—Provides that Congress may admit new states to the Union and restricts changes in boundaries of states.
5. Territorial Governance Clause—Authorizes Congress to govern territory of the United States.
6. Republican Government Clause—Provides that each state is to be guaranteed a republican form of government, and the national government will, when requested, help maintain domestic order.

E. Article V—Methods of Constitutional Amendment

1. Amendment may be *proposed* by two-thirds vote in both houses of Congress and *ratified* by legislatures of three-fourths of states (method used for all amendments except the twenty-first).
2. Amendment may be *proposed* by two-thirds vote in both houses of Congress and *ratified* by special ratifying conventions called in three-fourths of states (a method used only for the twenty-first amendment).
3. Upon application of legislatures of two-thirds of states, Congress *shall* call a convention for proposing amendments which are to be valid when ratified by the legislatures of three-fourths of states (a method never successfully undertaken).
4. Upon application of the legislatures of two-thirds of states, Congress *shall* call a convention for proposing amendments which are to be valid when ratified by conventions in three-fourths of the states (a method never successfully undertaken).

F. Article VI

1. Provides that debts created under the Articles of Confederation were to be honored.
2. Provides for supremacy of the Constitution, laws, and treaties of the United States over the constitutions and laws of the states.

G. Article VII

1. Ratification of the Constitution was to be by convention in the states, rather than by state legislatures.
2. Ratification by conventions of nine states required to make Constitution operative.

III. METHODS OF CONSTITUTIONAL CHANGE

A. Formal Amendment

1. Only twenty-six formal amendments were adopted in first 182 years, including ten amendments adopted in 1791.
2. Compared with other written constitutions, is difficult to amend formally.
3. Two methods of formal amendment have been used successfully, as indicated above.
4. National convention method has been unsuccessfully attempted at least twice in the twentieth century.

B. Informal Amendment

1. By acts of Congress.
   a. Congress cannot by itself formally amend Constitution.
   b. Congressional acts in fulfillment of constitutional provisions have, however, made significant changes in the Constitution.
   c. Judiciary Act of 1789, by creating a system of U.S. District Courts and U.S. Circuit Courts of Appeals, constituted an act of Congress in fulfillment of Article III.
2. By judicial interpretation.
   a. U.S. Supreme Court must often make interpretations in ruling on validity of state and federal laws and actions of public officials.
   b. Lower federal courts also must make interpretations.
   c. Supreme Court has been viewed as a perennial constitutional convention.
   d. Supreme Court decisions may make gentle or radical changes in meaning of the Constitution.
3. By custom.
   a. Practices on which the Constitution may be mute, but which are essential to the system of government.
      (1) Political parties.
      (2) Presidential nominating conventions.
   b. Have rounded out a complex governmental system under a simple but elastic Constitution.
4. By executive disposition.
   a. Courts are sometimes dependent on President for execution and enforcement of judicial decisions.
   b. President's attitude toward enforcement or non-enforcement may have effect on meaning of Constitution — temporarily or permanently.
   c. Dramatic examples are President Eisenhower's dispatch of U.S. Army forces to Little Rock, Arkansas, in 1957 to enforce federal court order directing integration of Little Rock High School; and President Jackson's refusal in 1832 to enforce a decision of the Court.
5. By public opinion.
   a. Eighteenth amendment, seeking to outlaw manufacture and sale of alcoholic beverages, was never uniformly enforced because of public hostility.
   b. Fifteenth amendment, seeking to outlaw racial discrimination in voting, was not enforced uniformly for many decades because of sectional public hostilities.

SELECTED TEST QUESTIONS

I. Multiple Choice

1. *Separation of powers* (checks and balances) is an expression referring to the division of powers: (a) between the states and the national government; (b) between the states and the counties; (c) between the states and the cities; (d) among the executive, legislative, and judicial branches of government.
2. The method of selecting United States Senators was changed by the: (a) nineteenth amendment; (b) twentieth amendment; (c) twenty-first amendment; (d) twelfth amendment.
3. When it was first introduced, the new Constitution drew much opposition from the: (a) shipping interests; (b) mercantile class; (c) lawyers; (d) agrarian and debtor classes.
4. The first twenty-five amendments to the United States Constitution were all *proposed* by: (a) action of legislatures in three-fourths of the states; (b) two-thirds vote in both houses of Congress; (c) action in legislatures of two-thirds of the states; (d) action in special conventions meeting in two-thirds of the states.
5. Authors of the Constitution provided that it was to become effective when: (a) ratified by legislatures of the thirteen states; (b) ratified by legislatures of nine states; (c) ratified by conventions in nine states; (d) ratified by conventions in thirteen states.

II. True-False

1. One prominent statesman who did not attend the constitutional convention was Thomas Jefferson.
2. A primary purpose for the writing of the Constitution was to promote democracy throughout the states.
3. The constitutional convention met as an open forum, where anybody could enter and offer his views.
4. In writing an entirely new Constitution, the Founding Fathers exceeded the stated intention of the Congress of the Confederation in its call for a convention.
5. The new Constitution won immediate acclaim from the vast majority of the people in the thirteen states.

CHAPTER 5

Federalism—An American Experiment

INTRODUCTION

One factor which helped bring about the American Revolution was a disagreement between colonists and the Crown over the extent of self-rule powers which should be placed in the hands of the colonists. If, as many colonial leaders maintained, the colonial legislatures should be given the power to control domestic policy, while the English Parliament retained authority over intercolonial and foreign matters, a division of sovereignty would have been the result. But it was commonly believed at that time that sovereignty (ultimate political authority) could not be divided. Subsequent developments in the British Commonwealth and in the United States of America might be interpreted as supporting the viewpoint of the colonists that sovereignty could be divided. For a division of sovereignty between or among two or more levels of government is the core feature of the theory of federalism.

The men who wrote the United States Constitution in 1787 invented federalism largely because they had no other practical choice. At the end of the Revolution, the thirteen states each held *all* the powers of government. The Articles of Confederation had not altered that centralization of power. The authors of the Constitution were trying to see to it that the new central government would be vested with powers essential for its existence, but powers which would not rouse uncompromising objections from the states or from the people who viewed state government as *their* government.

And yet, the federalism of 1789 is not the federalism of today. One cannot fail to be impressed by the structural and operational differences between the United States as a federal union in 1789 and the United States as a federal union today. To approach an understanding of that union, it might be best to first examine the forms of government with which the authors of the United States Constitution were familiar.

I. GOVERNMENTAL FORMS KNOWN BY THE FOUNDING FATHERS

A. Unitary Government

1. All governmental power centrally located.
2. Governmental power may be exercised by central agency or delegated to subdivisions created by central government.
3. Considered by many incompatible with democracy in 1787.
4. Known today to be compatible with democracy, partially because of technological advances (communications, travel, etc.).
5. England, a great democracy, has unitary government.
6. Each of American states was unitary in form upon separation from England. Other examples are France, Israel, and Philippines.

B. Confederation

1. Form of government experienced in America under the Articles of Confederation.
2. Characterized by decentralized governmental power.
   a. Sovereign states create central agency vested with limited powers in limited areas, while not necessarily sacrificing any real sovereignty.

    b. Central agency acts directly with states, but may have no direct power over people.

    c. So limited in power, central agency has hard time merely surviving.

  3. No existing examples today of confederations, with possible exception of the United Nations.

II. FEDERALISM IN THE UNITED STATES

A. Why It Was Invented

1. Because the states had *all* the power of government, and the people weren't willing to transfer *all* governmental power to an untried new agency. Unitary government was unacceptable.
2. Confederation had been tried under the Articles of Confederation for eight years and was unsatisfactory to many.
3. Unitary form was considered incompatible with the desired democracy.
4. Confederation considered too democratic by many.
5. A type of federalism is what the colonists had urged upon England before the American Revolution.
6. No apparent practical choice presented itself.
7. Federalism offered an opportunity to preserve the better features of both unitary and confederate forms.

B. Advantages Claimed for Federalism

1. Makes possible a government preserving the better features of both unitary and confederate forms.
2. Ideally suited to a large geographical area, since it encourages diversity in local government.
3. Avoids concentration of political power.
4. Satisfactorily accommodated the fact of existing state governments.
5. Suitable for heterogeneous people.
6. Encourages experimentation on state level (by one state) without risking loss growing out of failure of broad experiment.
7. States serve as training ground for national leaders.
8. Keeps government close to the people.

C. Disadvantages Inherent in Federalism

1. Rigidity inherent in a written constitution.
2. Complexity growing out of plural governments.
3. Duplication of offices and functions.
    a. Instead of one chief executive, the United States has 51.
    b. Instead of one judicial system, the United States has 51.
    c. Conflicts of authority.

III. CONSTITUTIONAL NATURE OF AMERICAN FEDERALISM

A. Federalism Defined

1. Divides governmental power (sovereignty) between or among two or more levels of government.
2. Requires written constitution.
3. Central government is sovereign in matters of general concern.
4. Local governments (states) are sovereign in matters of local concern.
5. Conflicts of authority inherent in thin dividing line between powers of central and local governments makes necessary an agency (such as the United States Supreme Court) with authority to resolve such constitutional conflicts.

6. National government supreme.
7. All governmental power limited.
   a. Article I, Section 8, limits powers of national government.
   b. Article I, Section 9, limits powers of state governments.
   c. U.S. Bill of Rights limits both state and national governments.
   d. Thirteenth amendment limits state and national governments, as well as individuals.
   e. Fourteenth amendment limits state governments.
   f. Fifteenth amendment limits state and national governments.

IV. DIFFICULT QUESTIONS OF AMERICAN FEDERALISM

A. Exactly Where Is the Dividing Line Between National Powers and State Powers?

B. Is the United States a Union of States or a Union of People?

C. To What Extent May the National Government Use Its Delegated Powers to Achieve Control of the Actions of Individuals?

V. IMPLIED POWERS VERSUS STATES' RIGHTS – MCCULLOCH V. MARYLAND (1819)

A. Facts Confronting the Supreme Court

1. Congress had chartered the Bank of the United States.
2. Maryland legislature had levied discriminatory tax against Baltimore branch.
3. McCulloch, officer of branch bank refused to pay tax and state sued.

B. Questions Confronting the Court

1. Since the Constitution is silent on the subject, does Congress have legitimate power to charter a bank?
2. If Congress does have the power to charter a bank, does a state have legitimate power to tax such an institution?

C. The Court's Answers to the Questions

1. Opinion written by Chief Justice John Marshall, dedicated nationalist.
2. Gave birth to concept of *implied powers* by stating that powers delegated to Congress *implied* power to charter a bank.
3. Said states lacked power to tax an instrumentality of the national government, since "the power to tax is the power to destroy."
4. Court's opinion served as great boost to concept of national supremacy and strengthened national government by stating that *implied* powers may grow out of limited powers granted by Constitution to the national government.

VI. FOREIGN AFFAIRS – INHERENT POWER

A. Nature of Inherent Powers

1. Universally acknowledged as belonging to all sovereign national governments.
2. Need no basis in constitution or statutes.

B. Examples of Inherent National Power

1. To acquire territory through discovery and occupation (a subject on which the United States Constitution is silent).

2. To make international agreements outside constitutional provisions for treaties.
3. To declare war (although this power is delegated to Congress by the U.S. Constitution).
4. To send and receive ambassadors (another power delegated to Congress by the U.S. Constitution).

C. Treaty-Making Power

1. President has power to make treaties.
2. Must have approval of two-thirds of Senate.
3. Constitution is supreme over treaties.
4. Treaty cannot abridge rights guaranteed by Constitution.
5. Treaties superior to state laws.
6. Supreme Court decision in *Missouri v. Holland* (1920) helped spell out the treaty-making power and the applicability of treaties.

VII. STATUS OF THE STATES IN THE FEDERAL UNION

A. Powers of the States

1. Reserved powers.
   a. Powers not granted by the U.S. Constitution exclusively to the national government nor denied to the states.
   b. Reserved to the states by the tenth amendment to the U.S. Constitution.
   c. Example of reserved power is the "police" power—power of the states to regulate individual behavior in the interest of health safety, morality, or general welfare of citizens.
2. Concurrent powers.
   a. Powers exercised by both state and national governments.
   b. Example is power to tax.
3. Prohibited powers.
   a. Powers denied the states or the states and national government.
   b. Commonest examples lie in the area of civil rights.
4. All limitations on state powers apply equally to political subdivisions of states, such as cities, counties, school boards, etc.

B. Constitutional Responsibilities of National Government to States

1. States guaranteed by Constitution *republican form of government.*
   a. *Republican* is vague term, but apparently would exclude monarchy or pure democracy.
   b. Determination and enforcement left to Congress when it seats or refuses to seat a state's congressional delegation.

C. Constitutional Interstate Obligations

1. Full-faith-and-credit clause.
   a. Requires states to enforce civil judgments rendered in courts of other states and accept public records of other states as valid.
   b. Does not apply to enforcement of criminal laws.
2. Privileges and immunities of citizens.
   a. States may not deny to citizens of other states—
      (1) Freedom to enter their states.
      (2) Full protection of the law.
      (3) Freedom to engage in lawful occupations.
      (4) Equal treatment in property and taxation with citizens of their own respective states.

      b. States may, however, deny citizens of other states —
        (1) Political rights.
          (a) Voting.
          (b) Public office.
          (c) Jury service.
        (2) Admission to publicly supported institutions.
    3. Methods of settlement of interstate conflicts.
      a. Interstate compacts.
      b. United States Supreme Court.

D. Supreme Court as Interstate Arbiter

    1. Serves to standardize state-administered justice throughout the states.
    2. Settles peacefully disputes among states.
    3. Insures supremacy of national laws.
    4. May review state administrative, executive, legislative, and judicial actions with power to nullify them as conflicting with Constitution, laws, or treaties of the United States.
    5. Decisions tend to favor national powers over state powers.

VIII. SHIFTING EMPHASIS TO NATIONAL POWER

A. Formal Constitutional Nature of American Federalism

    1. Has changed little since 1787.
    2. Constitution in 1787 created a framework for eventual development of a nation.
    3. Prior to Civil War, constitutional history was characterized by debate as to whether the United States was a union of states or a union of people.
    4. Northern victory in Civil War strengthened the position of nationalists at the expense of "states' rights" advocates.

B. Causes for the Growth of National Power

    1. Growth of business enterprises to national scope.
    2. Growth of labor unions and other associations to national scope.
    3. Increased and improved transportation and communications, which have reduced importance of state boundaries, placed greater demands on national government for attention.
    4. Demands of national defense.
    5. Demands of world trade.
    6. Nationalization of problems once considered of local importance only.
      a. Importance of the nation's physical health to national security considerations.
      b. Importance of nation's educational standards to national security.
    7. Limited tax resources of the states and resulting limited ability to cope with major problems.
    8. Increased confidence of many Americans in national government.
    9. Increased urbanization.
  10. Concentration of wealth.
      a. Example: Regulation of agricultural production by the allocation of farm price supports.
      b. Example: Regulation of minimum standards in highway construction by allocation of funds to states for road building.

SELECTED TEST QUESTIONS

I. Multiple Choice

1. The basic characteristic of federalism is:
   (a) democratic government; (b) centralization of powers; (c) centralized government; (d) division of sovereignty between or among two or more levels of government.
2. The Supreme Court's decision in the case of *McCulloch v. Maryland* gave birth to the concept of:
   (a) judicial review; (b) separate-but-equal; (c) implied powers; (d) state supremacy.
3. The agency of national government which has kept the Constitution applicable to changing conditions has been the:
   (a) chief executive; (b) Congress; (c) Supreme Court; (d) Federal Trade Commission.
4. A government in which all governmental power is vested in one central agency, there to be exercised or delegated, is called:
   (a) unitary; (b) confederation; (c) federation; (d) dictatorship.
5. Federalism was created by the authors of the American Constitution because:
   (a) it was considered the most efficient form of government; (b) it was the most democratic form; (c) it fitted the form of prevailing political theory; (d) it was the only practical choice.

II. True-False

1. At the time the Constitution was written, it was commonly believed by leading American statesmen that democracy had gone too far in the states.
2. One advantage claimed for federalism is the decentralization of governmental power which it makes possible.
3. A disadvantage of federalism is said to be the duplication of governmental machinery which it makes necessary.
4. Because a federal system of government draws a thin line between powers of the central and local governments, an agency such as the United States Supreme Court is considered necessary to resolve power disputes.
5. At the time the U.S. Constitution was written, a unitary national government was feared as a threat to democracy.

CHAPTER 6

Evolving American Federalism

INTRODUCTION

In Chapter 5, American federalism was described as a neat mechanical theory. The national government was said to be sovereign in certain areas of governmental concern, such as the regulation of interstate commerce. State governments were said to be sovereign in certain other areas, such as regulation of intrastate commerce and exercise of the police power. One writer has described this as the "layer cake" concept of American federalism. In the top layer are neatly compacted all the powers of the national government; in the bottom layer are found the separate and distinct functions and powers of state governments.

How nice it would be if the American federal system could be so easily and conveniently analyzed. But Professor Martin Grodzins of the University of Chicago has gone on to describe federalism *in practice* as more like a marble cake, with an intermingling of functions, than like a layer cake, with functions separate and distinct. This intermingling can be seen best perhaps by examining the example of railroad traffic. If it crosses a state line, it constitutes interstate commerce, coming under control of the national government. Rail shipments originating and ending within a single state constitute intrastate commerce, thus—the theory tells us—falling under regulation of state government. However, both the interstate and intrastate shipments may have moved over the same rails. In this simple example, one might easily read the urgent necessity for close cooperation between state and national governments. This need has not gone unrecognized by administrators of governmental programs at the state and national levels. Cooperation has become the hallmark of American government—cooperation among state, local, and national levels.

Nonetheless, national and state interests often conflict in the political arena. Pressures may be brought to bear on state legislators which differ from those felt by members of the national Congress. Disagreement over the proper division of powers between states and the national government often lies beneath a conflict of interests. But no "best" formula has been discovered for drawing a dividing line between state powers and national powers.

The men who wrote the United States Constitution did the best they could in the face of circumstances which confronted them at the time. The state-national power dispute has raged persistently ever since. What are "states' rights"? It is obvious that throughout United States history *states' rights* has arisen repeatedly as the anguished wail of any interest which felt it was being treated unsympathetically at a given moment by the national government. The source of the cry would seem to depend on whose ox is being gored.

I. DIVISION OF POWERS BETWEEN NATIONAL AND STATE GOVERNMENTS

A. Where to Draw the Line

1. Question cannot be answered scientifically, objectively.
2. Division is a political problem.

B. Balancing the Two Powers

1. Some view states as power necessary to counterbalance power of national government.

2. Some see states as dying unit of government, incapable of levying taxes adequate for the support of its institutions.

C. Growth of Government—National and State

1. Wrong to assume that when national power increases, state power declines.
2. Expansion of national government often strengthens states.
3. Improved machinery of government in many states urgently needed.

II. COOPERATION AMONG STATES (HORIZONTAL FEDERALISM)

A. When Interstate Compacts Are Used

1. Formerly used only to settle boundary conflicts between states.
2. More recently used to deal with economic, conservation, and service problems with interstate implications.
   a. Port of New York Authority established by compact.
   b. Education compacts.
   c. Water-pollution and water-use compacts.
   d. Oil and gas conservation by compact.
   e. Clemency compacts.
   f. Wildlife conservation by compact.

B. Informal Cooperation

1. Extradition.
2. Police radio networks.
3. Highway safety.
4. Regional conferences.

C. Effectiveness of Interstate Cooperation

1. Diversity of state laws is great handicap.
2. Common efforts by states in cooperative research efforts and cooperation in educational facilities have been described as highly successful.

III. COOPERATIVE FEDERALISM (VERTICAL FEDERALISM)

A. Grants-in-Aid

1. Provides for joint national-state operation of program.
   a. Washington provides part of money.
   b. State provides matching funds in varying proportions.
   c. Washington sets minimum standards.
   d. States administer programs.
2. Started in 1802, but has grown most rapidly in twentieth century.
3. Broadly utilized.
   a. For highways.
   b. For land-grant colleges.
   c. For many welfare programs.
4. Advantages.
   a. Utilizes superior revenue ability of national government toward a goal of national standardization.

b. Helps maintain decentralization of government.

c. Guarantees local administration within national standards.

d. Enables national government to participate in, and lend direction to, programs from which it might otherwise be constitutionally barred.

5. Criticisms of grants-in-aid.

a. Causes states to yield spending initiative in order to qualify for matching funds from Washington.

b. Proliferation of programs.

c. Complexity of national standards.

d. National programs often cause states to overlook more pressing local needs for which national funds are not available.

B. Tax Sharing

1. Plan to continue sending money from Washington to the states, but with greater freedom in the states to spend it within broader boundaries set by Congress.

2. Sometimes called the *Heller Plan* after its advocate, Walter Heller, Chairman of President Lyndon Johnson's Council of Economic Advisers.

3. Some critics say plan would weaken state governments by reducing their responsibility for revenue collection.

IV. THE THIRD CONTENDER: THE CITIES

A. Traditional Status

1. According to time-honored view of federalism, it implies a sharing of governmental power (sovereignty) between a national government and what Americans call *state* governments.

2. The city, a creature of the state, had no role in the federalism concept.

B. New Status

1. Many great cities have developed vital two-way communications with Washington, bypassing state governments.

2. Increasingly, funds have flowed directly from Washington to the cities.

a. Especially applicable to recent poverty programs.

b. Direct flow of funds to cities naturally displeases politicians at state level.

V. EVERYDAY WEAKNESSES IN AMERICAN FEDERALISM

A. Interstate Competition

1. Competition for business and residents discourages taxation on businesses and consumers.

2. Competition for industry discourages taxes or regulations on industry, encourages state subsidies.

3. Competition especially disastrous to conservation programs.

B. Law Enforcement

1. Problem aggravated by modern transportation methods.

2. State lines limit jurisdiction, but not travel.

3. Inability of state and local police to control criminals has led to clamor for national action.

4. Congress has used its commerce power to place limits on certain crimes, when they involve interstate commerce.

a. Theft.

      b. Kidnaping.

      c. Transportation of women for immoral purposes.

      d. Gambling information.

      e. Certain shipments of firearms.

   5. Enforcement of local laws and maintenance of peace remains almost exclusively a matter for state and local police.

C. Law Avoidance

   1. Avoidance of taxes.

      a. Cigarette taxes.

      b. Gasoline taxes.

      c. Other consumer taxes or transportable items.

   2. Avoidance of police regulation.

      a. Fugitive criminals.

      b. Legal abortion.

      c. Divorce requirements.

      d. Corporate charters.

SELECTED TEST QUESTIONS

I. Multiple Choice

1. "States' rights" is:

(a) a tight legal concept carefully defined in the United States Constitution; (b) a tight legal concept growing out of comparison of state and national constitutions; (c) a legal concept defined in state and national statutes; (d) a vague concept which may vary in meaning, according to who uses it.

2. "Cooperative federalism" is a term which describes:

(a) cooperation among the executive, legislative, and judicial branches of government; (b) cooperation among state governments to better resist encroachments by the national government; (c) competition among states to determine which can attract the most money from Washington; (d) cooperation among national, state, and local governments in financing and administering programs of interest to all.

3. A major advantage claimed for grants-in-aid is that they:

(a) keep the national government from spending too much money; (b) utilize the superior revenue capabilities of the national government; (c) restrict the national government to the kinds of activities specifically authorized by the Constitution; (d) prove that states are better qualified than the national government to plan and finance needed improvements.

4. The *Heller Plan* of tax sharing would:

(a) place tighter restraints on the states in their spending of national funds; (b) place tighter restraints on Washington in the appropriation of tax revenues; (c) free the states from many restrictions in their spending of shared national revenues; (d) cut off the sharing of federal tax revenues with the states.

5. A major weakness seen by some in the Heller Plan is that it would:

(a) encourage the states to neglect their tax-raising responsibilities; (b) increase state taxes; (c) restrict the states too narrowly in their planning of expenditures; (d) open the door to greater corruption in Washington.

II. True-False

1. Federalism in practice bears out the belief that state and national authority should be kept separate and distinct.
2. The interstate compact is used today primarily for settling boundary disputes.
3. Most enforcement of criminal laws is the responsibility of the national government.
4. Cities are sometimes considered a third factor in the concept of federalism.
5. Drawing the line between powers of state and national governments is a responsibility of the National Council of Governors.

CHAPTER 7

First Amendment Freedoms

INTRODUCTION

The men who wrote the United States Constitution did not write a bill of rights as part of that document. In all probability, a majority of them thought a bill of rights unnecessary for the kind of government they were creating. At any rate, the absence of a bill of rights aroused much suspicion among the people. Eager to see the Constitution ratified, the Federalists promised that once it was ratified, the first Congress would propose a bill of rights to be added to the Constitution as amendments.

In this manner, the Constitution was ratified. The first Congress in 1789 proposed twelve amendments to serve as a bill of rights. Ten of these amendments were ratified before the end of 1791 and are what is known as the United States Bill of Rights. The Bill of Rights established a relationship between individuals and their new national government. It drew lines across which this new government might not step. It served as a restraint on the national government, and in recent decades has served as a restraint on *all* government in the United States.

The most basic of all rights of individuals are protected *against governmental interference* by the First Amendment, which declares, "Congress shall make no law respecting an establishment of religion, or prohibiting the free exercise thereof; or abridging the freedom of speech, or of the press; or the right of the people peaceably to assemble, and to petition the government for a redress of grievances." These are—and always have been—the most basic rights of a free people.

In the first Congress, James Madison argued that the new Bill of Rights should protect individuals against encroachments by state governments, as well as the national government. But this proposal was rejected by Congress. State constitutions already had bills of rights, and few people had reason to be suspicious of state government.

But history was to demonstrate that it was the state governments—and not the national government—which constituted the most likely source of infringement of the basic rights of the people. State courts were not to prove vigilant in the protection of individual liberties.

One of the more dramatic chapters in American constitutional history deals with the "nationalization" of individual liberties—that is to say, the changing interpretation of the United States Constitution which has brought about the protection of individual liberties by the United States Bill of Rights against incursion *by either national or state governments.*

Briefly stated, this exciting change in significance of the Bill of Rights was made possible by ratification of the Fourteenth Amendment in 1868. The Fourteenth Amendment restrains the states exclusively, and has caused the United States Bill of Rights to be interpreted as restraining the states in much the same way as it restrains the national government.

Without an understanding of this basic fact, one would be hard put to understand the many sociopolitical revolutions brewing on the American scene today.

I. RELIGIOUS FREEDOM

A. Freedom of Belief

1. Implies absolute right to hold any or no religious belief.
2. Cannot be infringed as a qualification for holding public office.

B. Freedom to Advocate

1. Less absolute than freedom to believe.
2. Can be limited only when it poses danger of injury to rights of others.
3. Does not exempt individual from necessity to obey the law.

C. Freedom to Practice Religion

1. Less absolute than freedom of belief and freedom to advocate.
2. Does not sanction practice in violation of the law, such as polygamy, gambling, or draft evasion.

D. The Establishment Clause

1. Two interpretations:
   a. No-preference doctrine.
      (1) National and state governments forbidden to show preference to a particular religion.
      (2) Governments may act to help all religions.
   b. Separation doctrine.
      (1) Views Constitution as a "wall of separation" between church and state.
      (2) Government may not aid or support any or all religious organizations or activities.
      (3) Position adopted by the U.S. Supreme Court.
         (a) The Court in 1948 held unconstitutional the use of privately chosen instructors to teach religion in public-school classrooms during school hours (*McCollum v. Board of Education*).
         (b) In 1952, however, the Supreme Court found constitutional the practice of releasing pupils from school during school hours to receive religious instruction off the school grounds (*Zorach v. Clauson*).
         (c) In 1962 the Court ruled unconstitutional the required reading of nondenominational prayers in public school classrooms (*Engel v. Vitale*).
         (d) In 1963, the Court held that required reading of Bible verses in public-school classrooms violated the establishment clause (*Abington School District v. Schempp*).
         (e) The Court has upheld Sunday-closing laws, not as compelled observance of a religious holiday, but as providing a day of rest for working people.
         (f) Detailed application of the separation doctrine is a major constitutional dilemma facing judges and lawyers today.

II. FREEDOM OF SPEECH

A. Considered Essential in a Democracy

1. If man cannot criticize his government, how is his government to be improved?
2. Only through free expression of differing views can government be kept responsive to the people and qualify to be classed a democracy.

B. Essential in the Quest of Truth

1. In a democracy, there is no absolute truth; especially in politics, truth is relative, changing.
2. The best test of truth lies in the ability of an idea to win popular acceptance.
3. Some believe speech should be free only for those who agree with them, but this misses the point of free speech in a democracy.
4. Freedom of speech means freedom to tell a "lie"; the inaccuracy of today may be the truth of tomorrow.

5. The first amendment protects free speech against infringement by government; *tolerance* is required to protect the individual against suppression by his neighbors.
6. However, freedom of speech is not an absolute right.

C. Two Supreme Court Tests for Privileged Speech

1. Clear-and-present-danger doctrine.
    a. Formulated by Justice Holmes in his Supreme Court opinion in *Schenck v. United States* (1919).
    b. Holds that speech is protected by the Constitution unless its utterance creates a *clear and present danger* leading to substantive evils which Congress has a right to prevent.
    c. Justice Brandeis in 1927 elaborated on this doctrine by declaring that no danger flowing from speech can be clear and present, so long as opportunity exists for full discussion.
2. Dangerous-tendency doctrine.
    a. Was expressed by the Supreme Court in *Gitlow v. New York* (1925).
    b. Stems from common law, is thus much older than the clear-and-present-danger doctrine.
    c. Implies that government may outlaw speech which has *a tendency* to bring on a substantive evil.
    d. Leaves greater discretion to the legislative branch.

D. Preferred-Position Concept

1. Meaning.
    a. First-amendment freedoms take precedence when in conflict with other constitutional rights.
    b. Some have proposed that freedom of expression is an absolute right.
    c. Viewed as extension of clear-and-present-danger doctrine.
    d. Governmental limitations on free expression must be supported by showing of absolute necessity.
    e. In general, takes broad view of individual freedoms and narrow view of governmental right to regulate behavior.
2. Historical perspective.
    a. Was official view of the Supreme Court in the 1940s.
    b. Is minority view on the Court today, but is still supported by some justices.
3. Other constitutional criteria for free speech.
    a. Prior restraint.
        (1) Licensing.
        (2) Censorship by prior examination.
        (3) Banned as restraint on both oral and printed speech.
        (4) Freedom from prior restraint has not been made applicable to all communications media; movies, for example, are not fully protected.
        (5) Concept presumes invalidity of any law seeking to curb freedom of expression; burden of proving necessity falls on government.
    b. Vagueness.
        (1) Applies as measure for determining validity of any law seeking to curb first-amendment freedoms.
        (2) Standard assumes invalidity of any law "so vague that men of common intelligence must necessarily guess at its meaning. . . ."
        (3) Also means that laws must not be so vague as to allow administrators to discriminate against those whose actions they disapprove.

(4) Law forbidding "indecent behavior" would likely be considered by courts overly vague in the absence of tight definition of "indecent behavior," since prudent men may reasonably differ in their understanding of term.

   c. Overbreadth.

      (1) Closely related to *vagueness* concept.

      (2) Holds that laws legitimately affecting first-amendment freedoms may not be written or applied so broadly as to infringe protected behavior.

III. FREEDOM OF PRESS

A. Meaning

1. Freedom from prior restraint by government.
2. Protects newspapers, magazines, radio, television, books, pamphlets, but not necessarily movies.

B. Limitations

1. Does not imply free access to all information as a matter of right, although most *public* records unrelated to national security are available for inspection.
2. Does not exempt publisher from responsibility for publishing libel.

C. Libel

1. Defined by state laws and offenses triable in state courts.
2. Public officials have scant recourse to libel actions.
3. Professional entertainers, athletes, and other public figures have less than full recourse in libel actions.

D. Obscenity

1. Because it will not lend itself to objective standards, obscenity is one of the most difficult issues ever to confront the Supreme Court.
2. Three judicial standards.
   a. Contemporary community standards.
   b. Redeeming social value.
   c. Knowledgeable sale.
3. Regulation of obscenity.
   a. Primarily a matter subject to state control.
   b. Courts have demanded that obscenity laws be precisely drafted, so as to avoid undue vagueness and overbreadth.
   c. Relationship between obscene literature and obscene acts has never been established, but is repeatedly alleged.
   d. Congress has made it a crime to send obscene literature through the mails.
      (1) Postmasters have no authority to judge obscenity.
      (2) Supreme Court has held that use of mails is not a privilege the government may freely take away.
4. Status of motion pictures.
   a. Prior to 1952, they drew no protection from first amendment.
   b. Seven states and many cities subjected movies to prior censorship by boards with authority to ban public showings.
   c. In 1952, the Supreme Court extended some constitutional protection to motion pictures (*Burstyn v. Wilson*).

d. Films are still treated differently than printed media; movie censorship has not been held unconstitutional, but only grounds on which a showing can be banned is proof in court that the movie is obscene.

e. As a result of Supreme Court decisions, movie censorship, while not unconstitutional, has been rendered administratively impossible, for all practical purposes.

f. Censorship of movies, like that of books, has become a non-governmental matter growing out of pressures exerted on exhibitors — in the case of books, on booksellers.

E. Regulation of Radio and Television

1. National government exerts exclusive governmental control.
2. Regulation and assignment of frequencies is administered by Federal Communications Commission.
3. FCC has not attempted to censor political views, but has sought to insure "fairness" through equal-time principle.

F. Handbills and Pamphlets

1. Political and religious expression especially protected.
2. Advertising handbills also protected.

G. Picketing

1. Peacefully conducted, picketing is protected under the first amendment as a form of speech.
2. Is not protected when conducted for illegal purpose.
3. State laws may not validly ban picketing which involves infraction of no other state law.

H. Symbolic Speech

1. Action may constitute symbolic speech protected by the first and fourteenth amendments against governmental interference.
2. Burning of draft cards is not protected symbolic speech (*United States v. O'Brien*).
3. Wearing of black arm bands by public-school pupils in protest against the Vietnam War was held to be protected symbolic speech (*Tinker v. Des Moines Ind. School Dist.*).

IV. FREEDOM OF ASSEMBLY

A. Scope

1. Protects the right to assemble peaceably in private homes or public places.
2. Does not imply a right to incite riots, block traffic, destroy property, or interfere with legitimate public functions, such as the meeting of school classes.
3. Governments may license parades which use the public streets only by precisely drawn regulations, fairly administered.

V. CONGRESSIONAL EFFORTS TO OUTLAW SEDITION

A. Sedition Act of 1798

1. Politically inspired by Federalists.
2. Banned malicious criticism of the government or its officers.
3. Was so unpopular that it helped defeat Federalists in the election of 1800.

B. Sedition Act of 1918

1. World War I measure.
2. Made criminal act any criticism of the government, Constitution, flag, soldiers, or uniform of the United States.
3. Aimed at curbing speech, rather than action.

C. Smith Act of 1940

1. First sedition act since 1798 to apply in peacetime.
2. Made criminal act advocacy of the overthrow of the government with intent to cause overthrow of government.
3. Aimed primarily at totalitarian movements in the United States.
4. In 1951, the Supreme Court upheld legality of the act *(Dennis v. United States)*, but in 1957 narrowly restricted its scope.

D. Internal Security Act of 1950

1. Outlaws conspiracies to establish totalitarian dictatorship in the United States.
2. Strengthened sedition and espionage laws.
3. Restricted migration to the United States of Communist aliens.
4. Aimed primarily at the Communist party in the United States.
5. Required registration of Communist organizations in the United States.

E. Communist Control Act of 1954

1. Denied the Communist party the right to run candidates for office.
2. First time in U.S. history Congress has outlawed political party.

VI. LOYALTY OATHS

A. Nature

1. Intended primarily after World War II to place curbs on Communists, especially in public employment.
2. Consist of a positive declaration of loyalty to nation.

B. Applicability

1. Have commonly been required of civil servants, military personnel, schoolteachers, college teachers and students, recipients of research grants and fellowships.
2. Signed under pain of perjury.

VII. SUBVERSION CONTROL IN A DEMOCRACY

A. What Is Subversion?

1. Much disagreement surrounds question.
2. Many laws, statutes, and executive orders on the subject have been loosely worded and imprecisely aimed.

B. Dangers of Anti-Subversion Legislation

1. Laws often written in atmosphere of inordinate fear.
3. Has tendency to force conformity in speech, thought, and behavior.
3. Laws sometimes cater to intolerant factions, impatient with mere dissent.

SELECTED TEST QUESTIONS

I. Multiple Choice

1. The men who wrote the Constitution included no bill of rights because they thought it would be:
   (a) too democratic; (b) not democratic enough; (c) too radical; (d) unnecessary.
2. The first amendment, like the rest of the Bill of Rights, serves today as a restraint on:
   (a) the national government only; (b) state governments only; (c) all government in the United States; (d) individuals only.
3. The fourteenth amendment serves to restrain:
   (a) the national government only; (b) state governments only; (c) state and national governments; (d) individuals only.
4. First-amendment freedoms take precedence over other constitutional rights when exposed to the:
   (a) No-preference doctrine; (b) preferred-position doctrine; (c) separation doctrine; (d) vagueness standard.
5. Libel is an offense defined by:
   (a) the United States Constitution; (b) national statute; (c) state statutes; (d) municipal ordinance.

II. True-False

1. Freedom of the press implies freedom from prior restraint.
2. Motion pictures receive the same protection under the first amendment as do newspapers and books.
3. The Supreme Court has held movie censorship unconstitutional.
4. Freedom of the press implies free access to *all* governmental information and records as a matter of right.
5. The government exercises no more regulation over radio than it does over newspapers.

CHAPTER 8

Equality and Equal Protection

INTRODUCTION

In spite of the ringing rhetoric in the Declaration of Independence about the equality of all men — and in spite of a historic striving for human equality which extends back far beyond the Declaration of Indpendence, the harsh fact remains that only in recent decades has the national government in the United States undertaken to seriously pursue the goal of human equality for all persons.

Who would deny that blacks have been subjected to systematic patterns of racial discrimination throughout the land, or Mexican-Americans in the Rio Grande Valley area, or orientals on the West Coast, or Jews and a multitude of ethnic groups on the East Coast.

And yet, since 1791, the fifth amendment of the U.S. Constitution has proudly proclaimed that no person shall "be deprived of life, liberty, or property, without due process of law," this constituting a limitation on the national government. And since 1868, the fourteenth amendment has declared that, "No State shall make or enforce any law which shall abridge the privileges and immunities of citizens of the United States; nor shall any State deprive any person of life, liberty, or property, without due process of law; nor deny to any person within its jurisdiction the equal protection of the laws." The fifth amendment limits both national and state governments. The fourteenth amendment limits state governments only.

How difficult it is today to believe that our national and state governments could have ignored these mandates for equality, acquiescing and even joining in the national pattern of racial discrimination which was known in every quarter of the land right up to the midpoint in the twentieth century.

It may be a useful metaphor to say that the fifth and fourteenth amendments have served as the primary modeling clay used by the federal courts to mold the foundation for a new pattern of racial justice in the United States. But this would be an oversimplification. The new era in civil rights was brought about by a combination of independent actions by the executive, legislative, and judicial branches of government.

I. THE THREE CIVIL WAR AMENDMENTS

A. Thirteenth Amendment

1. Outlaws all slavery in the United States.
2. Authorizes Congress to force an end to slavery by statute.

B. Fourteenth Amendment

1. Provides the first and only constitutional definition of U.S. citizenship.
2. Defines citizenship so as to include newly freed slaves.
3. Forbids states to deny citizens the *privileges and immunities* of United States citizens, but without undertaking to describe those privileges and immunities.
4. Forbids states to "deprive any person of life, liberty, or property, without *due process of law.*"
5. Forbids any state to "deny to any person within its jurisdiction the *equal protection* of the law."

C. Fifteenth Amendment

1. Forbids voting discrimination against United States citizens because of race, color, or previous condition of servitude.
2. Restrains both national and state governments.

D. Congressional Action

1. Congress enacted laws (known as the Civil Rights acts) seeking to achieve the aims of the fourteenth amendment.
2. National policy was directed toward elevating the newly freed blacks to a status of full citizenship.

II. CIVIL RIGHTS DISILLUSIONMENT

A. Political

1. Northern political leaders abandoned Negro cause.
2. Public opinion, North and South, opposed full equality.
3. Presidents after Lincoln were unwilling or unable to push Negro cause.
4. Congress refused to expand Negro rights or protect Negro rights already assured by the Constitution, but often ignored in fact.
5. Blacks were systematically denied the ballot in Southern states and some sections of the North, in violation of the fifteenth amendment.
6. Racial segregation became the established pattern in most parts of the United States.

B. Judicial

1. The Supreme Court, in the **Civil Rights Cases** (1883), declared unconstitutional the Civil Rights Act of 1875, which outlawed racial discrimination in public places, ruling that the fourteenth amendment was intended to curb **state** action, not **individual** action.
2. In *Plessy v. Ferguson* (1896), the Supreme Court sustained state laws requiring racial segregation.

C. Social

1. Blacks were denied most jobs, other than menial.
2. Blacks were denied educational opportunities.
3. Racial segregation became a locked-in pattern of life.
4. Public opinion generally accepted the black as inferior to the white person.

III. THE ASCENT FROM MENIALITY

A. Northward Migration

1. By World War I, some trends toward racial equality in education and employment were noted in Northern states.
2. Southern blacks began a northward migration, settling in industrial cities, where they gained political influence through the ballot.
3. Northward migration was accelerated by opportunities for industrial employment during World War II.
4. Movement of industry into the South led to unionization and improved status for Southern blacks.
5. A black middle class developed, sensitive to color discrimination.

B. Executive Response

1. The Presidency was the first branch of national government to respond to mounting pressures from blacks for an end to official color discrimination.
   a. Enfranchised, Northern urban blacks constituted an important bloc vote which could sometimes swing a state's vote in the electoral college.
   b. Recognizing importance of Negro support, Presidents responded to Negro pressures to appoint federal judges sympathetic to the black cause.
   c. Roosevelt's New Deal programs had some built-in bars to racial discrimination.
   d. Roosevelt created Fair Employment Practices Commission in 1941 to eliminate racial discrimination in national defense employment.
   e. Under pressure from black leaders, President Truman in 1948 banned racial discrimination in the armed forces.

C. Judicial Response

1. Supreme Court took the lead in reinterpreting the fourteenth amendment to make it an effective barrier against official discrimination by states, thus reversing earlier Supreme Court decisions.
2. In the 1930s, 1940s, and 1950s blacks won important court victories striking at racial discrimination in voting, education, and interstate transportation.

D. Some Reasons Why Congress Lagged on Reform

1. Important congressional committees were disproportionately controlled by Southern congressmen who opposed civil rights legislation.
2. Disproportionate rural representation had some tendency to muffle representation of the urban black.
3. In the Senate, Southerners could filibuster civil rights legislation to death.
4. Prior to 1950, there existed little clamor among whites for civil rights reforms.
5. Northern congressmen were disinclined to offend their Southern colleagues in the absence of political feasibility.

E. Congressional Response

1. Overriding a Southern filibuster in the Senate to enact the first civil rights legislation in more than 80 years—the Civil Rights Act of 1957, designed to secure voting rights for blacks.
2. The Civil Rights Act of 1960 was designed to further guarantee the voting rights of blacks.
3. In the Civil Rights Act of 1964, Congress outlawed discrimination *by individuals* in places of public accommodation or in employment practices, strengthened its ban on voter discrimination, and expedited school desegregation.

F. Integration in Education

1. Supreme Court decisions.
   a. Beginning with its decision in the case of *Missouri ex rel Gsines v. Canada* (1938), the Supreme Court issued a number of decisions striking at the legitimacy of racial segregation in tax-supported higher education.
   b. By its revolutionary decision in the case of *Brown v. Board of Education* (1954), the Supreme Court overruled the "separate-but-equal" doctrine as it applied to public schools and in effect ordered racial integration of all tax-supported schools.
2. Acts of Congress.
   a. Following the Supreme Court's school-integration decision in 1954, Congress accepted the illegality of public-school segregation, acknowledging integration as the new rule of law in several appropriations measures.

b. In the Civil Rights Act of 1964, Congress provided for the withholding of appropriated funds for public education from states which failed or refused to integrate public schools.

IV. BLACK POWER — THE NEW MILITANCY

A. The Gradualist Viewpoint

1. The blacks have now been granted essential *legal* equality.
2. A gradual process of social adjustment must be awaited before further steps toward full equality can be effectively undertaken.

B. The Black Dilemma

1. Having won a large degree of political equality through a series of voting-rights laws, many blacks are eager to maximize this power.
2. Other blacks, suspicious of civil rights "handouts," are militantly eager to get on with the job of bringing about racial equality.

C. Violence in the Cities

1. The 1965 Watts riots in Los Angeles.
2. 1967 Detroit riots.
3. In 1966 and 1967, race riots afflicted many of the nation's cities.

D. The Kerner Commission on Civil Disorders

1. Appointed by President Johnson in 1967 to investigate causes of disorders and to recommend solutions.
2. Blacks on commission were all moderates.
3. Commission found that United States was "moving toward two societies, one black, one white — separate and unequal."
4. It recommended "action on an unprecedented scale to increase opportunities for blacks — especially in jobs, education, and housing."

V. TWO SUPREME COURT CASES — BEGINNING AND END OF LEGAL SEGREGATION OF RACES

A. *Plessy v. Ferguson* — Birth of the "Separate-but-Equal" Doctrine

1. Decision written by the Supreme Court in 1896 upholding Louisiana law requiring segregation of races on railroad cars.
2. Provided legal support for segregation of races in public places, *enforced by state laws* for 58 years.
3. Fact that facilities provided for blacks often were not equal to those for whites was ignored by enforcement agencies.

B. *Brown v. Board of Education* — Death of the "Separate-but-Equal" Doctrine

1. Followed many minior victories by black leaders in chipping away at the "separate-but-equal" concept.
2. Was the first frontal assault on the legitimacy of segregated schools by organized black leaders.
3. Confronted the Supreme Court with the question of whether racial segregation in tax-supported schools was of itself a violation of equal protection clause of the fourteenth amendment.

4. Supreme Court ruled unanimously that separate facilities in tax-supported schools, when required by law, could not be equal.
5. Court declared compulsory segregation of children in public school solely on basis of race was a denial of equal protection; laws requiring such segregation were thus ruled unconstitutional.
6. Court ordered public-school authorities to proceed to end racial segregation in the tax-supported schools.
7. Many schemes to avoid school integration have since been struck down by federal courts.
8. Public school segregation, legally required on the basis of race alone, still exists in some areas of the nation today, but is unconstitutional because of the 1954 Supreme Court decision.

VI. VOTING RIGHTS FOR BLACKS

A. Efforts to Bar Blacks from the Ballot

1. White primaries.
2. "Grandfather clauses."
3. Racial gerrymandering.
4. Denial of equal legislative representation.
   a. In state legislatures.
   b. In the U.S. House of Representatives.
   c. In local governmental bodies.
   d. Often took the form of rural overrepresentation and underrepresentation of cities, where large numbers of blacks lived.
5. Discriminatory literacy tests.
   a. Administered by whites.
   b. Aimed at arbitrarily denying blacks the ballot.
6. Intimidation.
7. Efforts to exclude blacks from the polls were employed most commonly in Southern states.

B. National Efforts to End Voting Discrimination by States

1. *Fourteenth amendment.*
   a. Second of three Civil War amendments, ratified in 1868.
   b. Defined citizenship so as to include blacks.
   c. Forbade states to deny any citizen *privileges and immunities* of national citizenship.
   d. Was rendered ineffective for nearly a century by combination of Supreme Court decisions and racial ruses employed by states, primarily in the South.
2. *Fifteenth amendment.*
   a. Third of three Civil War amendments, ratified in 1870.
   b. Aimed specifically at guaranteeing Negro voting rights.
   c. Restrains both national and state governments from restricting right of United States citizens to vote "on account of race, color, or previous condition of servitude."
   d. Was rendered largely ineffective for nearly a century by combination of Supreme Court decisions and racial ruses employed by states, primarily in the South.
3. *Civil Rights Acts of 1957 and 1960.*
   a. Placed major responsibility for ending voting discrimination on U.S. district courts.
   b. Authorized U.S. district judges to appoint registrars to register black voters after a pattern of discrimination had been discovered.
4. *Civil Rights Act of 1964.*
   a. Outlawed literacy tests for those who can prove six years of schooling.
   b. Outlawed literacy tests in federal elections and banned oral literacy tests.

5. *Voting Rights Act of 1965.*
   a. Virtually banned literacy and understanding tests as prerequisite to voting.
   b. Authorized direct intervention by federal registrars to guarantee voting rights of blacks.
   c. Was directed specifically at areas in which racial discrimination in voting persisted.
   d. Authorizes U.S. Attorney General to appoint poll watchers.
   e. Provides criminal punishment for officials or individuals who intimidate person seeking to vote.

C. **Recent Trend in Negro Voting in the South**

1. More than half of eligible black voters now registered in each Southern state.
2. In some areas economic and social pressures have replaced legal measures to keep blacks from voting.
3. Impact of increased Negro voting has been especially felt in Southern cities.
4. Election of Negro candidates to public office has shown sharp increase.

VII. LEGAL ASSAULT ON RACIAL DISCRIMINATION BY INDIVIDUALS

A. **Action by States**

1. Most states have enacted statutes against racial discrimination by individuals in places of public accommodation.
2. Most states forbid racial discrimination in public employment.
3. Many cities ban discrimination by landlords.
4. Enforcement of anti-discrimination statutes by state governments has often been lax.

B. **Action by the National Government**

1. Some backers of fourteenth amendment in 1860s viewed its ratification as authority for the national government to outlaw racial discrimination by individuals.
2. By the *Civil Rights Act of 1875,* Congress outlawed racial discrimination by individuals in places of public accommodation (public transportation, lodgings, theaters, etc.).
3. Supreme Court, in the *Civil Rights Cases* (1883) overruled the Civil Rights Act of 1875, holding that Congress had no authority to bar racial discrimination by individuals.
4. By executive order, President Franklin D. Roosevelt in 1941 banned discrimination in employment by national-defense contractors.
5. President Truman in 1948, by executive orders, ended segregation in the armed forces and discrimination in federal employment.
6. With the Civil Rights Act of 1964, Congress committed the national government to a comprehensive effort to end racial discrimination by individuals in public accommodations and employment.

VIII. DISCRIMINATION IN HOUSING

A. **Nature of the Problem**

1. Racial discrimination in housing was a problem primarily in the cities, where Negro ghettos or slums developed as segregated sections of the community.
2. Racial discrimination in housing was supported in many states by restrictive real estate covenants, in which property owners mutually agreed not to sell property to certain minority groups.
3. Resulting segregation in housing barred blacks from the suburbs, and made school integration almost impossible.
4. Bar against blacks in the suburbs was caused largely by policies of real estate and financial agencies.

B. Assault on the Problem

1. In the 1968 case of *Shelley v. Kraemer,* the Supreme Court ruled that state courts could not be used to enforce restrictive covenants.
2. *Civil Rights Act of 1968* prohibits racial discrimination in rental or sale of 80 percent of housing in the United States.
3. Supreme Court decision in *Jones v. Mayers* (1968) ruled that Congress had illegalized racial discrimination in housing by an act of 1866, and that this act was binding.

SELECTED TEST QUESTIONS

I. Multiple Choice

1. In the United States Constitution, slavery is outlawed by the:
   (a) first amendment; (b) thirteenth amendment; (c) fourteenth amendment; (d) fifteenth amendment.
2. The only definition of citizenship in the United States Constitution is found in:
   (a) Article I; (b) the fifth amendment; (c) the fourteenth amendment; (d) the fifteenth amendment.
3. The equal protection clause of the fourteenth amendment restrains:
   (a) the national government; (b) state governments and their subdivisions; (c) state and national governments; (d) individuals only.
4. A state law requiring racial segregation on railroad cars was sustained by the United States Supreme Court in the case of:
   (a) *Plessy v. Ferguson;* (b) *Brown v. Board of Education;* (c) *Shelley v. Kraemer;* (d) *Jones v. Mayers.*
5. The "separate-but-equal" doctrine governing racial segregation by state law was overturned by the Supreme Court in:
   (a) the *Civil Rights Cases;* (b) *Brown v. Board of Education;* (c) *Shelley v. Kraemer;* (d) *Jones v. Mayers.*

II. True-False

1. The major interest in protecting individual rights of citizens has rested with the national government throughout our constitutional history.
2. The national government may, under certain conditions, assign federal registrars to register voters.
3. Passage of national laws banning voting discrimination has been followed by a noticeable increase in registration of black voters.
4. In the case of *Shelley v. Kraemer,* the Supreme Court ruled that state courts could not enforce restrictive real estate covenants.
5. In spite of obvious disinterest by the President and the federal courts, Congress has assumed an aggressive leadership in protecting the rights of the American Negro.

CHAPTER 9

Citizenship, Rights, and Property

INTRODUCTION

National citizenship was a dim concept in the early decades of American history. No definition of national citizenship was included in the Constitution written by the Founding Fathers in the summer of 1787. After that, the subject simply did not arise with any great frequency. State citizenship was the important thing, and this was a matter for definition by state constitutions and statutes.

Until the middle of the nineteenth century, the question of national citizenship remained fairly moot. Then, in 1857, the Supreme Court, in one of its earliest commentaries on national citizenship, ruled that neither a state nor the national government could confer national citizenship on native-born citizens, either slave or free. This opinion came in the decision of the Court in the famous Dred Scott case, which was later to be described as a "public calamity." One can readily appreciate the dilemma of freed slaves prior to the Civil War, left without constitutional guidance to ponder their status in American society.

Following the Civil War Congress proposed, and in 1868 the states ratified, the fourteenth amendment. The first sentence of the fourteenth amendment undertakes to define citizenship in these simple words: "All persons born or naturalized in the United States, and subject to the jurisdiction thereof, are citizens of the United States and of the State wherein they reside."

This language of the fourteenth amendment was clear enough to any who wished to understand it to underscore the fact that the Supreme Court's Dred Scott decision had been overruled—that American-born blacks were in fact United States citizens.

Immediately following its definition of United States citizenship, the fourteenth amendment proceeds with a language often interpreted to establish the supremacy of national citizenship over state citizenship: "No State shall make or enforce any law which shall abridge the privileges and immunities of citizens of the United States. . . ." It was demonstrated in the preceding chapter that a combination of Supreme Court decisions and state laws, reinforced by public apathy, was used to forge an effective detour around these constitutional provisions in many parts of the United States for nearly a century.

But this begs the question. What are the "privileges and immunities" of citizens of the United States? No simple answer to this question can be offered. However, a considerable amount of evidence bearing on the subject may be advanced to help one who seeks an answer to the question.

While the constitutional definition of citizenship embraces the concept of *jus soli*—citizenship according to place of birth—the United States Congress has expanded the admission to United States citizenship to include persons who are not "born or naturalized in the United States." Congressional qualifications for citizenship—unlike the constitutional qualification—is based on the principle of *jus sanguinis*—citizenship by blood relationship. Thus three possible avenues are open to United States citizenship: (1) native birth; (2) naturalization; and (3) overseas birth to one or two parents of American citizenship.

I. THREE POSSIBLE RELATIONSHIPS OF INDIVIDUAL TO THE UNITED STATES

A. Citizen

1. Bears primary responsibility for conduct of public affairs.
2. Has all rights, privileges, and immunities recognized by the Constitution.

B. Alien

1. Resident of the United States, but citizen of another nation, or else person without citizenship in any nation.
2. Remains in the United States at the will of Congress.

C. National

1. Owes allegiance to United States.
2. Is entitled to protection by the United States, but lacks full citizenship.
3. Natives of some U.S. territories are nationals.

II. DUAL CITIZENSHIP

A. Causes

1. Grows out of a conflict between national citizenship rules of *jus soli*—place of birth—and *jus sanguinis*—blood relationship.
2. May result when a citizen of a nation adhering to the rule of *jus sanguinis* bears a child in a nation observing principle of *jus soli;* by two different laws, offspring is a citizen of two different nations.

B. Solution

1. Dual citizenship conflicts commonly resolved by treaty.
2. In absence of treaty, affected person usually lives by law of place of presence.

III. ACQUIRING UNITED STATES CITIZENSHIP

A. By Constitutional Provision

1. Principle of *jus soli* is prescribed.
2. Citizenship may be acquired by either birth or naturalization.
3. Persons subject to United States jurisdiction at time of birth recognized as citizens.
4. U.S. citizens also citizens of state in which they reside.
5. State laws cannot nullify U.S. citizenship by birth.
6. U.S. citizenship recognized as superior to state citizenship.

B. By Act of Congress

1. Statutory provisions for citizenship complicated.
2. Principle of *jus sanguinis* is prescribed.
3. Major purpose is to provide citizenship for children born abroad to American parents.
4. If one parent is citizen, the other alien, citizen-parent must have lived in United States or possession ten years, five since age of fourteen, and child must live in United States five years between ages of fourteen and twenty-eight.

C. By Naturalization

1. Standing of aliens.
   a. Owe temporary allegiance to country in which present.
   b. Must pay taxes, same as citizens.
   c. Enjoy most rights of citizens in regard to property, business, governmental services, and relationship to state.
   d. May not vote, hold public office, practice certain professions or receive certain welfare-type benefits.

2. Laws governing naturalization.
   a. Under Articles of Confederation, each state had own laws concerning naturalization.
   b. Because of conflicts which arose under state laws of nationalization, authors of the Constitution granted Congress power "to establish an uniform rule of nationalization."
   c. Since 1790, Congress has exercised exclusive jurisdiction over naturalization.
   d. Certificates of naturalization may be issued by either federal or state courts.
   e. *Immigration and Nationality Act of 1952 (McCarran-Walter Act).*
     (1) Passed over veto of President Truman.
     (2) Placed political-based restrictions on immigration of aliens to the United States.
3. Group naturalization.
   a. May be accomplished by act of Congress to make citizens of large numbers of people.
   b. Has been used to "blanket in" natives of most American territories.
4. Qualifications for naturalization.
   a. Evidence of lawful entry.
   b. Good moral character.
   c. Ability to use English language.
   d. Knowledge of American government.
   e. Acceptance of American governmental standards.
   f. Must not be polygamists, armed forces deserters, draft evaders, anarchists, Communists, totalitarians.
   g. Must renounce any titles of nobility.
   h. May be pacifists.
   i. Minimum age of eighteen.
   j. Five years' residence in the United States and six months' residence in state where petition is filed.
5. Loss of citizenship.
   a. Any citizen may renounce citizenship.
   b. Naturalization may be revoked on proof naturalization was obtained by deception.
   c. Citizen abroad may renounce citizenship before American diplomatic official.
   d. Citizen living in the United States may renounce citizenship only in time of war.
   e. Congress has claimed power to revoke citizenship as a criminal penalty, but the Supreme Court has ruled otherwise.
6. Rights of citizenship.
   a. To vote, if qualified by law to do so.
   b. To use navigable waters of United States.
   c. To assemble peacefully.
   d. To petition national government for redress of grievances.
   e. To be protected by national government on high seas.
   f. To travel freely throughout the United States.
   g. Possible to travel freely outside the United States (although Congress and the President have indicated otherwise, and courts have not ruled definitively).
   h. To live in the United States.

IV. CONSTITUTIONAL RIGHT TO PROPERTY AND CONTRACT

A. Reasons for Constitutional Interest

1. One of basic purposes for writing the Constitution was to make property and contracts secure from encroachments by state government.
2. Articles of Confederation provided no protection for property or contracts.

B. Constitutional Protections

1. Article I, Section 10, of the United States Constitution forbids the states to impair the obligation of contract.
   a. States may not extend periods for payment of debts under private contract.
   b. States are bound by own contractual obligations.
   c. Privileges granted by corporate charters are contractual obligations and must be observed by states.
2. Due process.
   a. The fifth amendment forbids the national government to deprive any person of life, liberty, or *property* without due process of law.
   b. The fourteenth amendment forbids any state to deprive any person of life, liberty, or *property* without due process of law.
   c. *Due process of law* has never been comprehensively defined by the U.S. Supreme Court.
   d. Due process clauses are the bases for much litigation in federal courts.
3. Two kinds of due process.
   a. *Procedural* due process, a concept related primarily to criminal law, refers primarily to methods used by government in confronting and trying a criminal suspect.
   b. *Substantive* due process relates to the "reasonableness" of law, serving primarily as a restraint on legislatures.

C. Legitimate Government Controls on Property

1. By *zoning* property, governments may restrict use which may be made of real property.
2. *Eminent domain* is a concept which gives government the right to take private property for public purposes after paying a fair price.

V. CONSTITUTIONAL PROTECTION OF INDIVIDUALS FROM GOVERNMENT

A. Unreasonable Search and Seizure

1. Fourth and fourteenth amendments restrain all law officers from making unreasonable searches and seizures.
2. In quest of criminal evidence, lawmen are restrained from entering private premises without search warrant issued by competent court.
3. Fourth amendment provides that warrants will not be issued on mere suspicion, "but upon probable cause, supported by oath or affirmation."
4. Warrant must specifically describe the place to be searched "and the person or thing to be seized."
5. Some circumstances are exempted from warrant requirement.
   a. Automobile may be searched without warrant if search is incident to a lawful arrest.
   b. Automobile may be searched without warrant if police have reason to believe it contains contraband.
   c. Police may frisk a person for weapons when there is reason to believe individual is armed and dangerous.
   d. Police may not lawfully search person on mere suspicion.
6. Evidence seized in illegal searches are not admissible in court.
7. Wiretapping and use of electronic eavesdropping devices come under the purview of the fourth amendment, but definite standards remain to be developed by the courts.

B. Freedom from Coerced Confessions

1. Fifth amendment provides that no person may be compelled to testify against himself in criminal prosecutions.
2. Presumption of innocence of accused places burden of proof on the prosecutor.
3. Although the Constitution prescribes this protection in criminal *prosecutions,* it is also observed in civil actions.
4. In some cases, government may compel testimony by granting witness immunity from prosecution on basis of his testimony.
5. Coerced confessions are inadmissible in court.
6. The U.S. Supreme Court in the 1950s and 1960s played an aggressive role in tightening standards in criminal prosecutions and protecting the rights of individuals accused of crime.
7. Congress, in the Crime Control Act of 1968, undertook to limit protections for criminal suspects spelled out by the Supreme Court.

C. Freedom from Illegal Detention—Habeas Corpus

1. Habeas corpus is an order by a court of competent jurisdiction directing one who has custody of an individual to present his ward in court for an examination of the legality of custody.
2. Is a guarantee written into Article I of the U.S. Constitution by the Founding Fathers.
3. Only Congress may suspend right of habeas corpus—and only in time of invasion or rebellion.
4. Executive suspensions of habeas corpus have been overruled by Supreme Court.

D. Ex-Post-Facto Laws

1. Retroactive *criminal* laws working to the disadvantage of the individual. Examples:
   a. Law making crime of an act performed before law was enacted.
   b. Law increasing penalty for an act performed before law was enacted.
2. Retroactive *civil* laws are not forbidden. Examples:
   a. Zoning ordinances.
   b. Tax increases.
3. Congress is forbidden to enact ex-post-facto laws by Article I, Section 9, of the U.S. Constitution.
4. States are forbidden to enact ex-post-facto laws by Article I, Section 10.

E. Bills of Attainder

1. Bill of attainder is a legislative act which would punish specified individuals without judicial trial.
2. Rare in U.S. history.
3. Congress is forbidden to enact bills of attainder by Article I, Section 9, of U.S. Constitution.
4. States are forbidden to enact bills of attainder by Article I, Section 10.
5. Primary objection to bills of attainder is obvious denial of due process of law, thus an invasion of the judicial function.

SELECTED TEST QUESTIONS

I. Multiple Choice

1. The law of citizenship determined by place of birth is known as:
   (a) *jus soli;* (b) *jus sanguinis;* (c) *jus civile;* (d) *jus gentium.*
2. The law of citizenship determined by blood relationship is known as:
   (a) *jus soli;* (b) *jus sanguinis;* (c) *jus civile;* (d) *jus gentium.*

3. *Procedural* due process is a concept related primarily to:
   (a) civil law; (b) international law; (c) statute law; (d) criminal law.
4. *Substantive* due process serves as a restraint on:
   (a) legislatures; (b) courts; (c) administrators; (d) policemen.
5. Unreasonable searches and seizures are restrained by:
   (a) Article I of the United States Constitution; (b) the first and second amendments; (c) the fourth and fourteenth amendments; (d) the fifth and sixth amendments.

II. True-False

1. The principle of eminent domain gives government the right to take private property for public purposes after paying a fair price.
2. An automobile may be searched without a warrant if police have reason to believe it contains contraband.
3. The burden of proof in a criminal prosecution falls on the accused.
4. The President may legally suspend the right of habeas corpus, but only in time of invasion or rebellion.
5. An *ex-post-facto* law is a retroactive *civil* law working to the disadvantage of the individual.

CHAPTER 10

Public Opinion

INTRODUCTION

The theory underlying representative democracy implies government which complies with the will of the people, or at least the will of a majority of the people. But a major problem of democracy is posed by the task of determining the will of the people. How are the elected officials to know what is the public will? Since a population numbering more than 200 million cannot be expected to all share identical opinions, how is government to deal with sharp differences of opinion? To what extent, if any, should the elected government undertake to mold public opinion? At any rate, how are the people's representatives supposed to know what the people want?

These problems go beyond the realm of democratic theory. They pose very real questions confronting the people's elected representatives every day. Beyond the question of what the people want lies the question of what the people will tolerate from their government. What of the elected representative of the people who is convinced that he knows better than his constituents what is in the interest of the nation and in the interest of the constituents themselves. Assuming the improbable — that he knows what his constituents want — does he dare to act on the impulse of his better judgment and his greater familiarity with the problems of government? Does he dare to vote the people's interest, rather than the people's will. Can he trust his mail to give him a fair representation of what the people want in the first place? These are all difficult questions confronting the elected representative in a democracy.

I. CHARACTERISTICS OF PUBLIC OPINION IN POLITICS

A. Quantitative Characteristics

1. No one public opinion.
2. As many opinions as individuals.
3. Politicians must make generalized groupings of individual opinions based on assumptions of vital individual interests.

B. Some Basic Influences on Individual Opinions

1. Economic status.
2. Social status.
3. Occupation.
4. Educational or intellectual status.
5. Group identification.

C. Stability of Political Opinion

1. Some political opinions are firmly held, not subject to ready alteration.
   a. Identification with a political party is a stabilizing influence.
   b. Party identification tends to color one's interpretation of events.
2. Dramatic events can cause dramatic shifts in opinion.

D. Qualitative Characteristics

    1. Intensity of opinions.
        a. Varies with individuals.
            (1) Some opinions firmly held.
            (2) Some opinions tentatively held.
            (3) Many individual attitudes are passive.
            (4) Intensity difficult to measure.
    2. Latency of opinions.
        a. Some opinions are firmly formed, ready to inspire action.
        b. Some opinions are latent, needing the cue of an event to bring them to life.
        c. Crisis can rouse latent opinion to a quest for action.
        d. Most opinions are probably vague and indefinite.

II. SOURCES OF POLITICAL OPINIONS

A. Basic Attitudes

    1. Family.
    2. School.
    3. Church.

B. Specific Political Values

    1. College.
        a. Formal instruction.
        b. Broader campus environment.
    2. Spouses.
    3. Mass media.
        a. Newspapers.
        b. Television.
        c. Radio.
        d. Magazines.
        e. Books.
        f. Movies.

III. PROPAGANDA

A. Defined: Propaganda Is Communication Disseminated in a Deliberate Effort to Influence (Public) Opinion in a Predetermined Manner

B. Some Basic Characteristics

    1. Closely related to education.
    2. Most education contains some propaganda.
    3. Effectiveness depends on constant repetition.
    4. Can be used to promote good and bad causes.
    5. Is an essential tool in political campaigning.

C. Some Propaganda Techniques

    1. Testimonial.
    2. Appeal to authority.

3. Glittering generality.
4. Card stacking.
5. Transfer.
6. Plain folks.

IV. THE MASS MEDIA

A. Daily Newspapers

1. Medium of declining competition.
2. Concentration of ownership and control has led to standardization of newspaper content, including editorials.
3. Promotional activities to sell papers and advertising thought by some to debase quality of product.
4. "Big-business" nature of daily newspaper publishing has caused daily newspapers to be predominantly conservative in management and editorial outlook.
5. Proposals for press reform.
   a. Establishment of voluntary codes of practice.
   b. Governmental intervention to promote competition.

B. Radio and Television

1. Unlike newspapers, the broadcast media are regulated and licensed by the national government *(Federal Communications Commission)*.
2. Must serve the public interest in order to be licensed.
   a. FCC may refuse license to stations not serving the public interest.
   b. FCC may not censor program content or interfere with freedom of speech conveyed by radio and television.
   c. FCC discourages concentrated ownership or control of broadcast outlets.
   d. FCC's "fairness doctrine" requires equal exposure to different sides in political campaigns or controversies.
   e. Broadcasters may air editorials, but must make time available for rebuttal.

V. MEASURING PUBLIC OPINION

A. Election Results

1. Rarely provide reliable measure of opinion on issues, since election campaigns are seldom waged on the basis of issues.
2. Candidates rarely take clear-cut stands on issues.
3. Several issues, in addition to the candidate's personality may blend together to influence the voter's behavior.

B. Public Opinion Polls

1. Used in the United States for more than a century.
2. Greatly improved in recent decades.
3. Polling techniques.
   a. Random sampling.
   b. Quota sampling.
   c. Weighted sampling.

4. Sampling limitations.
   a. Selecting a reliably representative sample.
   b. Phrasing the questions to avoid bias.
   c. Selecting unbiased interviewers.
   d. Estimating reliability of responses.
   e. Accurately interpreting results.

SELECTED TEST QUESTIONS

I. Multiple Choice

1. Concentration of ownership has led to noticeable standardization of content in:
   (a) newspapers; (b) magazines; (c) radio; (d) television.
2. Broadcast media are regulated and licensed by the:
   (a) Federal Communications Commission; (b) Interstate Commerce Commission; (c) Federal Radio Commission; (d) the Department of Justice.
3. Concentration of ownership has been accompanied by declining competition among:
   (a) radio stations; (b) daily newspapers; (c) television networks; (d) all media.
4. The "big-business" nature of daily newspaper publishing has caused daily newspapers in their editorial outlook to become predominantly:
   (a) radical; (b) liberal; (c) conservative; (d) none of these.
5. Through the Federal Communications Commission, the national government places some controls on the content of:
   (a) newspapers; (b) magazines; (c) radio and television; (d) billboards.

II. True-False

1. The Federal Communications Commission forbids untrue advertisements in newspapers.
2. Although newspapers are free of censorship, the Federal Communications Commission carefully censors the content of radio and television programs.
3. It is relatively easy for politicians to know what their constituents are thinking.
4. Opinion researchers have found it difficult to measure the intensity of opinions.
5. Election results rarely provide a reliable measure of opinion on public issues.

CHAPTER 11

Voting and the Voter

INTRODUCTION

Many well-qualified men (and women) seek elective political office in the United States at all levels of government. Very often the voter is expected to make a choice, not between a "good" candidate and one or more "bad" candidates, but between two or more persons who have all the credentials required of the office they seek. A good deal of mystery has always surrounded the question of what makes a majority or plurality of voters mark their ballots in favor of one candidate over the others who offer themselves for the office. In an ideal society, it might be possible to say that the sovereign voters base their voting behavior—their choices among candidates—on the policy issues brought out and publicized during the campaign. But in the American system of government, it is seldom possible for the voter to make his choice on the sole basis of real issues. Although little is known about the political behavior of man, it is well known that several factors are important in determining how the individual voter marks his ballot.

Many theories have been advanced to explain the true nature of the election in a democratic society. Numerous theories have been advanced, too, to explain the basis of decision by the individual American voter when he enters the election booth. But practical political experience has been hard on the theories.

Many scholars have undertaken systematic studies aimed toward revealing the mysteries of voting behavior—or at least some of them. Political scientists, sociologists, psychologists, anthropologists, and statisticians have exerted, and are exerting, tireless efforts toward the development of reliable research techniques to help with the objective measurement of factors contributing to the behavior of voters—both individually and in large numbers. Foremost among these techniques are questionnaires, intensive studies of election statistics, polls, interviews, and detailed studies of selected campaigns. Some advances have been made, and more may be expected to follow.

A major difficulty encountered in the study of political behavior grows out of the fact that political attitudes change. They sometimes change slowly, sometimes abruptly, sometimes temporarily, sometimes permanently. It is into the nature and causes of such change that many scholars have directed their efforts.

I. WHO BOTHERS TO VOTE?

A. Historical View of the American Franchise

1. Steady effort to qualify more persons to vote.
   a. Originally right to vote was limited to small group of property owners.
   b. Today the great majority of citizens who have reached the age of eighteen may qualify to vote in all elections.
   (1) Property qualifications were abandoned in first half of nineteenth century.
   (2) Blacks were legally enfranchised by ratification of the fourteenth amendment (1868) and the fifteenth amendment (1870) and by subsequent acts of Congress, but enforcement of their franchise has remained a continuing struggle.

(3) After several states had granted women the right to vote, this right was extended to women throughout the United States by ratification of the nineteenth amendment (1920).

(4) States were forbidden to deny the right to vote on account of age to persons who have reached their eighteenth birthday by ratification of the twenty-sixth amendment to the U.S. Constitution in 1971.

2. But, still, fewer than 70 percent of the qualified voters cast ballots.

a. Percentage of voter participation in the United States lags behind figures for many overseas peoples.

(1) Participation declined in early 1900s.

(2) Participation increased in the 1930s.

(3) Participation is greatest in presidential elections, greater in congressional elections than in local elections.

(4) Restrictive state election laws and administrative practices have discouraged voting.

(5) Lack of interest discourages voting.

B. Who Is Likely to Vote?

1. Higher-income person.
2. The college-educated.
3. The middle-aged.
4. Men.
5. Party enthusiasts.

C. Which Elections Arouse Voter Enthusiasm?

1. Presidential elections attract greatest voter turnout.
2. Off-year congressional elections rank second in voter appeal.
3. Local elections usually have smallest turnout.
4. Chief Executive contests attract more voters.

a. More votes are cast for U.S. representatives in presidential election years than in off-year elections.

b. More votes are cast in state elections when a governor is being chosen than in off-year legislative elections.

5. Two-party contests attract larger voter turnout than no-contest elections.

D. Proposals to Increase Voter Turnout

1. Raise educational standards.
2. Increase general level of economic well-being.
3. Improve the image of "politics."
4. Shorten the ballot in state and local elections to reduce the number of obscure elective offices.
5. Reduce the number of referendums required in state and local elections.
6. Simplify registration requirements.
7. Make political parties more competitive.

II. HOW AMERICANS VOTE

A. As Individuals

1. Party switching is easy and thought of as common among "fickle" American electorate.
2. However, party regularity — even by succeeding generations of a family — is a common characteristic.

3. Party "regulars" give each major party a reliable base in national elections.

4. "Independent" voters create major element of uncertainty in national elections.

B. Historical Voting Patterns

1. State patterns.
   a. Some states, like Maine and Vermont, have voted Republican in presidential elections with great consistency.
   b. Other states, like Mississippi and South Carolina, have been similarly consistent in supporting Democratic presidential nominees.
   c. Most states are considered "doubtful" by both parties.
2. Sectional patterns.
   a. The "Solid South."
   b. Not-so-solid border states.
3. The national trend.
   a. Reflects in most states a rise in the national popularity of the party.
   b. National tides often overwhelm local currents.
4. Straight-ticket versus split-ticket voting.
   a. More than half the voters vote for all the nominees of one political party—that is, they vote a "straight ticket."
   b. Straight-ticket voting enables one strong candidate on a party's slate to draw votes to the weaker candidates, thus it is said that weaker candidates ride into office "on the coattails" of the strong candidate.
5. Pattern of voting cycles.
   a. Some students of voting behavior have identified political trends which extend over longer period of time than a single term of office and which form a pattern of repetition.
   b. Theories based on these observations are considered of little value in predicting the outcome of any particular election.
   c. At least three underlying causes may be advanced to help explain the phenomenon of political cycles—if, indeed, they do exist.
      (1) Business and general economic conditions in the nation.
      (2) General employment conditions.
      (3) The international situation.

III. UNDERSTANDING VOTING BEHAVIOR

A. Some Basic Factors Influencing Individual Voting

1. Party identification.
2. Personality of candidates.
3. Family political attitudes.
4. Friends' political attitudes.
5. Political attitudes in peer groups.
6. Race.
7. Religion.
8. Income level.
9. Place of residence.

B. The Independent Voter

1. At least 25 percent of American voters do not identify consistently with one political party, are thus tagged "independent."

2. Some independents say they "vote for the man, rather than the party."

3. Some voters consider independent label more respectable than identification with any one party, but vote for candidates of one party with some consistency.

4. Younger, more prosperous, better educated voters are believed most inclined to identify selves as independents.

5. Vote of independents is considered important factor in determining election results.

6. Independent status is probably unrelated to political sophistication.

C. Campaign Effects

1. Election campaigns convert relatively few voters.

2. Campaigns reassure voters in their convictions.

3. Campaigns heighten political activity and increase voter turnout.

4. Those who are converted by campaign appeals are considered important segment of electorate in strong, two-party contests.

D. Active Political Participation

1. Degrees of active political participation.
   a. Leaders.
   b. Rank-and-file voters.
   c. Inactives.

2. Measurement of extent of participation is difficult.

E. Characteristics of the Political Activist

1. Political environment.
2. Psychological quest.
   a. The extrovert.
   b. The born-to-lead personality.
3. Public-policy involvement.
4. Social-occupational status.
   a. Professional persons are activist-prone.
   b. Farmers are relatively immune.
   c. Union members have been demonstrated to be activist-prone.
5. Factors influencing active political participation resemble those which influence people to vote.

F. Democratic Election Requirements

1. Election administration.
   a. Voter must be offered a choice.
   b. Secret ballot must be assured.
   c. Polling places must be conveniently located.
   d. Polling places must be impartially administered, free of partisan pressures.
   e. Equally weight ballots.
2. Voter registration.
   a. As number of voters grew, personal recognition of voters was sometimes impossible—especially in large cities.
   b. Ruthless political machines in large cities sometimes "floated" squads of voters from one precinct to another to repeatedly cast their ballots.
   c. Voter registration was developed in an effort to end multiple voting and voting by unqualified persons.

      d. Registration requirements have sometimes been used to discourage political participation by racial and ethnic groups.

   3. Election districts.

      a. The *precinct* is the basic geographical unit.

      b. In some areas the precinct stands alone as polling district; elsewhere precincts may be subdivisions of city wards or rural townships.

      c. Each precinct contains a polling place—commonly a schoolhouse, fire station, or other public building.

      d. Geographical size of precinct should be restricted enough to bring polling place within easy access of all voters living in it.

      e. Precincts are commonly designed to include between 200 and 1,000 voters.

      f. Major political parties commonly attempt to maintain a party organizer—"chairman"—within each precinct.

      g. Many politicians consider the precinct the level of political organization at which elections are won or lost.

   4. Election officials.

      a. Large number of officials are designated to preside over precinct voting place on election day.

      b. Selected on partisan basis, with state law commonly requiring that both parties be represented.

G. How the Individual May Be an Active Participant

   1. By keeping himself informed on matters of public interest.

   2. By seeking to form opinions based on facts.

   3. By voting.

   4. By attending precinct meetings of party of his choice.

   5. By studying qualifications of candidates for office.

   6. By volunteering to do part-time work for party or candidate of his choice.

   7. By contributing what he can afford to help pay campaign costs of his preferred candidate for office.

   8. By helping with party-organization work within his precinct.

   9. By asking officeholder to explain policies he does not understand.

  10. By discussing with others political issues on which he has informed himself.

SELECTED TEST QUESTIONS

I. Multiple Choice

1. The property qualification for voting was abandoned:
(a) with ratification of the thirteenth amendment; (b) during the first half of the nineteenth century; (c) with ratification of the seventeenth amendment; (d) with congressional passage of the Voting Rights Act of 1965.

2. Blacks were constitutionally enfranchised by ratification of the:
(a) thirteenth amendment; (b) fifteenth amendment; (c) sixteenth amendment; (d) nineteenth amendment.

3. Women were constitutionally enfranchised by ratification of the:
(a) fifteenth amendment; (b) sixteenth amendment; (c) seventeenth amendment; (d) nineteenth amendment.

4. As a general rule, the largest number of voters turn out for a:
(a) congressional election; (b) presidential election; (c) gubernatorial election; (d) municipal election.

5. The proportion of voters who vote the straight ticket is:
   (a) about one-third; (b) nearly 90 percent; (c) about three-fourths; (d) more than half.

II. True-False

1. Most states are considered "doubtful" by both parties insofar as voting behavior is concerned.
2. "Independent" voters create a major element of uncertainty in national elections.
3. At least one-fourth of American voters are considered "independents."
4. Election campaigns convert relatively few voters.
5. Precincts are commonly designed to include about 10,000 voters.

CHAPTER 12

Interest Groups in Politics

INTRODUCTION

It has been said with some exaggeration that when two Americans meet on a streetcorner in London, the first thing they do is form an association. The humorous intent of this anecdote is obvious, but the simple fact remains: Americans are widely known as joiners. No intelligent estimate can be made of the number of interest groups in existence in the United States. An *Encyclopedia of Associations* has been published with listings of 12,500 national associations representing almost every interest imaginable.

An interest group is a formal organization of people who share one or more common concerns and who exert a joint effort to try to influence some type of events—usually the formation and administration of public policy—law, that is—so as to protect or advance their common interests. Such organizations differ widely. They are large and small, permanent and temporary, rich and poor, powerful and weak. It would be difficult to imagine a group interest which is not represented in the nation's capital by one or more such organizations. The interests of college and university students, for example, are represented in Washington by at least a dozen or so such formal associations, although few college students are aware of any of them.

Charlie Rice, a newspaper columnist, has published his "hit parade" of associations, in which he selects some of the more unusual ones: "The Academy of Underwater Arts and Sciences, The Flemish Giant Breeders, The Hickory Handle Association, The Society of Grain Elevator Superintendents, The Technical Council for Airplane Hangar Doors, The Halibut Association of North America, The Flying Dentists of America, The Society of Smokers, The Society of Non-Smokers, The National Soup Mix Association, The National Poetry Lovers Association, and the National Toilet Seat Manufacturers Association."

Interest groups are organized at the national, state, and local levels, and many of them undertake to influence governmental policy at these levels. One person may belong to a number of such organizations, and it is difficult to imagine a person so isolated from the mainstream of society that he could avoid membership in at least one such group. Such associations necessarily represent the interests of many nonmembers, however. The predominant pattern in the United States has been for the formal organization of interest groups which represent the interests of producers, rather than consumers.

Some writers take a broad enough view of interest associations as to include such groups as the family and the neighborhood.

I. EXAMPLES OF INTEREST GROUPS

A. Business- and Producer-Oriented Associations

1. National Association of Manufacturers.
2. United States Chamber of Commerce.
3. National Agricultural Chemical Association.
4. National Association of Retail Merchants.

B. Professional Associations

1. American Medical Association.
2. American Bar Association.

3. American Dental Association.
4. American Association of University Professors.

C. Associations of Institutions

1. American Council on Education (colleges, universities, and educational organizations).
2. National Council of Churches (Protestant and Eastern Orthodox bodies).

D. Patriotic Organizations

1. Daughters of the American Revolution.
2. American Legion.

E. Organizations of Service Veterans

1. American Legion.
2. Veterans of Foreign Wars.
3. Disabled American Veterans.

F. Religious Interest Groups

1. National Council of Churches.
2. National Catholic Welfare Council.
3. American Jewish Committee.

II. HISTORICAL PERSPECTIVE

A. Farm Organizations

1. Probably the oldest occupational associations.
2. *The National Grange.*
   a. Earliest national farm organization in the United States.
   b. Organized in nineteenth century, shortly after Civil War.
   c. Known formally as *Patrons of Husbandry.*
   d. Was effective in leading farm demonstrations against low farm prices, railroad monopolies, and economic exploitation of farmers.
   e. Achieved many of its goals of state and national legislation to benefit farmers.
   f. In twentieth century, has become smaller, more conservative organization.
3. *American Farm Bureau Federation.*
   a. Largest farm group today.
   b. Organized in 1920 out of a movement started before World War I.
   c. Greatest strength is in the prosperous corn belt.
   d. Growth was aided by government agents working at the county level.
4. *National Farmers Union.*
   a. Founded in Texas in 1902.
   b. Most liberal of U.S. national farm groups today.
   c. Primarily represents small farmers with family-sized operations.
   d. Major strength is in the plains states.
5. Many specialized farm organizations represent single-crop interest of farmers.

B. Labor Organizations

1. Local unions are as old as the nation.
2. First effective national organization was the *Knights of Labor.*
   a. Organized at Philadelphia, Pennsylvania, in 1869.

  b. Was shrouded in secrecy because of employers' opposition.

  c. Membership rose to 700,000.

3. *American Federation of Labor* was organized before end of nineteenth century.

  a. Basic approach was to organize workers by crafts and skills.

  b. Was a confederation of strong national unions.

  c. Became dominant U.S. labor organization early in twentieth century.

4. *Congress of Industrial Organizations.*

  a. Unions representing coal miners and other industrial workers split away from the AFL and formed the CIO in the 1930s.

  b. Signed up both skilled and unskilled workers.

  c. After first operating within the AFL, the CIO was expelled in 1937.

5. Merger.

  a. AFL and CIO merged in 1955, adopting the name, *American Federation of Labor and Congress of Industrial Organizations (AFL-CIO).*

  b. Membership today exceeds 13 million.

C. Black-Power Groups

1. *National Association for the Advancement of Colored People.*

  a. Established in 1910 as the first successful American Negro interest group.

  b. Devoted to the use of litigation to end discrimination and win for blacks the right to vote.

  c. Generally considered the most important Negro interest group.

  d. Has more than 500 chapters today.

2. *National Urban League.*

  a. Promotes better relations between blacks and whites in the United States.

  b. Works for economic benefits to blacks—equal opportunity in employment, housing, and educational, health, and welfare services.

3. *Southern Christian Leadership Conference.*

  a. Organized by the late Dr. Martin Luther King.

  b. Dedicated to nonviolent actions, it sponsored may sit-ins and other peaceful demonstrations by blacks.

4. *Congress of Racial Equality.*

  a. Founded at Chicago in 1942.

  b. Largely a university-oriented organization.

  c. Has used nonviolent action to oppose racial segregation in the United States, such as "freedom rides" and sit-in campaigns.

  d. One of the more militant of the Negro-rights organizations.

III. ELEMENTS OF INTEREST-GROUP POWER

A. Membership

1. Size.

2. Unity.

3. Geographic concentration.

4. Enthusiasm.

5. Conflicting interests.

B. Degree of Members' Interest

1. Members on payroll usually active and keenly interested.

2. Hard-core members, though limited in numbers, are usually deeply involved.
3. Rank-and-file members are commonly difficult to interest.

C. Other Power Factors

1. Organizational structure.
   a. Some groups have informal structure, with authority dispersed.
   b. Some groups have *federal* form of organization, with authority divided between units and a central agency.
   c. Some groups are *unitary* in structure, with all real authority resting in a central agency and units performing as the central agency wishes.
2. Leadership.
   a. Usually held by small group long identified with the organization.
   b. Usually control administrative machinery.
   c. Often have power to discipline members.
      (1) By withholding services.
      (2) By expulsion from membership.
   d. May control the group's publications and propaganda.
3. External influences.
   a. Relationships with government and government officials.
   b. Economic environment.
   c. Public opinion.
   d. Strength of allied groups.
   e. Strength of opposed groups.

IV. TOOLS OF INTEREST-GROUP INFLUENCE

A. Propaganda

1. Word of mouth.
2. Television, newspaper, radio.
3. All other mass media.

B. Electioneering

1. In spite of nonpolitical postures, many powerful interest groups from time to time become politically active in a partisan sense.
2. Interest groups normally seek to cooperate with both parties.
3. While group's official position may remain neutral, its leaders often take a partisan position.
4. Members may volunteer time to help with campaign chores for the organization's preferred candidates.

C. Lobbying

1. One of the basic purposes of many interest groups.
2. Many corrupt practices of lobbyists in the nineteenth century have left lobbying with a tainted image in the public eye.
3. More than 1,000 active lobbyists are in Washington today.
4. Lobbyists also work at state and local levels of government.
5. Most lobbyists are attorneys.

6. A major role of the lobbyist is providing reliable information to lawmakers about specialized interests represented by the lobbyists.
7. Lobbyists also specialize in producing "grass roots" pressures on lawmaking bodies.

D. Litigation

1. Effective source of relief when political channels are closed.
2. Extent of use of courts depends on nature and aims of group.
3. Has proved especially effective avenue for causes of questionable popularity.
4. Courts have been used with increasing frequency in recent years by groups cut off from political relief.
5. Two types of action have been common.
   a. Lawsuits.
   b. *Amicus curiae* (friend of the court) brief, in which the group may formally support one side in an action in which it is not a party.

E. Peaceful Direct Action

1. Boycott.
2. Picketing.
3. Passive resistance.
4. Mass demonstrations.
5. Sit-ins.
6. Strikes.
7. Advertising and propaganda.

F. Violent Protest

1. Used in the United States as early as the Whiskey Rebellion in 1794, later in the Civil War.
2. Often used in frustration or in dissatisfaction with the status quo.
3. For many years was common in labor disputes.
4. Common student involvement is more recent in United States.
5. Has been common in situations of racial unrest.
6. Attracts attention of mass media and dramatizes causes.

V. BASIC CRITICISMS OF INTEREST GROUPS

A. Becoming Too Strong

1. Charge leveled at business interest groups in nineteenth century and early twentieth century.
2. In recent decades, the charge of bigness has been aimed at labor and farm groups.
3. However, the more members an interest group has, the greater the number of counter-pressures represented in its membership.

B. Oligarchical in Command

1. Leaders are said to abandon interests of members.
2. Abandonment of democratic ideals in leadership often charged.
3. However, **somebody** must serve as leader, and rank-and-file members are usually apathetic.

C. Interest Groups Do Not Represent All the People

1. Unquestionably, some groups do have disproportionate power.
2. Some groups—notably consumers—have had little or no representation by interest groups.
3. Under-organized Americans are free to form their own organizations, or else resort to the polls.

4. "Countervailing power" of interest groups with conflicting goals keeps any one group from becoming dangerously powerful, because the interests of some groups are served only at the expense of other groups.

SELECTED TEST QUESTIONS

I. Multiple Choice

1. The oldest occupational associations are believed to be:
   (a) labor unions; (b) farm organizations; (c) professional associations; (d) industrial associations.
2. The earliest farm organization in the United States was:
   (a) the Grange; (b) the Farm Bureau Federation; (c) the Farmers Union; (d) none of these.
3. The first effective national labor organization in the United States was:
   (a) the Knights of Labor; (b) the American Federation of Labor; (c) the Congress of Industrial organizations; (d) the International Brotherhood of Railway Trainmen.
4. The national organization whose policies are most likely to agree with those of the United States Chamber of Commerce is the:
   (a) AFL-CIO; (b) NAACP; (c) National Association of Manufacturers; (d) Southern Christian Leadership Conference.
5. The oldest national interest group working for Negro rights is the:
   (a) Urban League; (b) NAACP; (c) Southern Christian Leadership Conference; (d) Congress of Racial Equality.

II. True-False

1. The Urban League has been one of the more militant Negro-rights organizations.
2. One interest group which has been poorly organized and represented historically is the American consumer.
3. Generally speaking, lobbyists and interest associations in Washington are often helpful to congressmen.
4. Most interest groups steer clear of avowed affiliation with political parties.
5. Organized labor gained much power during the ferment of the 1930s.

CHAPTER 13

Political Parties

INTRODUCTION

Political parties are a part of the vital machinery of government—even though the men who wrote the United States Constitution did not see fit to make any mention of them there. Parties may be identified with "partisan" politics, and partisan politics may be frowned on by many unsophisticated people. But the simple truth is that partisanship is essential in a democracy, and without parties, our system of government would be faced with many stumbling blocks.

Parties provide a rallying point, around which like-minded people may gather in a democracy in effective pursuit of political goals. At the same time, parties provide a thread of continuity of political values running through our national history. It is no surprise that identification with a political party has been identified with political stability of the individual.

The political party has been defined as a voluntary association of voters whose purpose in a democracy is to control the policies of government by electing to public office persons of its membership. Ideally, one might wish to say that the main aim of a party is to provide a vehicle through which voters might associate in an effort to control public policy. But in the American system, policy is presented to the voters only in a vague sense, and the voter has little assurance that the man he supports for office will represent his policy interests in government.

One writer has described the political party as a kind of political interest group. And so it is—the main difference being that the interest group is probably more assured of some community of interest by practically all of its members than a political party is. Different people see different facets of a political party, support it or oppose it for broadly different reasons.

At any rate, the party does provide an instrument which any voter may use with varying degrees of success to register his endorsement of, or protest against, what he considers to be the policy trend of a specific group of political leaders in public office.

I. FOUR PARTY PERIODS IN AMERICAN HISTORY

A. The Borning Era

1. *The Federalists.*
   a. Movement for a strong central government.
   b. Origin may be traced to the debates of the constitutional convention in 1787.
   c. Leader was Alexander Hamilton, Washington's Secretary of the Treasury.
   d. Wanted sound financial policies by national and state governments.
   e. Greatest appeal was to mercantile interests—bankers, traders, shippers, and tradesmen.
2. *The Republican party.*
   a. Organized behind Thomas Jefferson and James Madison.
   b. Was united in opposition to President John Adams.
   c. Following included laborers, small farmers, frontiersmen, debtors.

B. The First Era of the Democrats

1. Republican leaders gradually drifted away from Jefferson's anti-aristocratic philosophy.

2. Under leadership of *Andrew Jackson,* the Democratic party emerged as successor to Jefferson's Republican party.

3. Democrats remained dominant in American party politics until split by the slavery issue before the Civil War.

C. Rise of the Republican Party

1. Republican party was founded in 1854, attracting a following of farmers, laborers, and small businessmen.

2. Party was first considered radical with its grass-roots appeal.

3. In 1860, *Lincoln* became first President elected by Republican party, opposing further expansion of slavery, favoring homestead land grants, and liberal wages for workingmen.

4. After Civil War, Republicans remained dominant for six decades, their homestead program winning support of land-hungry immigrants and farmers, high-tariff policies winning support of industrial interests and factor workers.

5. After the Civil War, the national Democratic party persisted as the opposition party, electing only two Presidents in a 70-year period.

   a. During these decades, the "solid South" developed as the most reliable stronghold of Democrats.

   b. Democrats during this period became identified with goals of low tariffs and states' rights.

6. Both parties remained moderate during period.

7. Major split in Republican party between conservative followers of President Taft and progressive Theodore Roosevelt facilitated election of Woodrow Wilson, first Democratic president in the twentieth century.

8. Republican coalition of interests during era included a strong Protestant following and "dries" — those who opposed legal sale of alcoholic beverages.

9. Democratic coalition included urban, Catholic, and "wet" voters.

D. The Great Depression and Democratic Revival

1. *Franklin D. Roosevelt,* Democratic governor of New York, led the Democratic party's return to national political dominance when he was elected President in 1932. First President to break the two-term tradition, Roosevelt was successful in seeking election to third and fourth terms.

2. Roosevelt's election to the presidency was accompanied by firm Democratic control of Congress and strengthening of the party in most states.

3. Democratic ascendency under Roosevelt was facilitated by widespread unemployment and economic stress of the Great Depression.

4. Roosevelt and his Democratic Congresses offered the "forgotten man" a "New Deal" — an innovative welfare-oriented policy direction by the national government.

5. Roosevelt pulled together a Democratic coalition of farmers, workingmen, Southerners, blacks, Catholics, the unemployed, ethnic and racial minorities, and many middle-class voters.

6. On Roosevelt's death in 1945, Vice President Harry S. Truman rose to the presidency, then was elected to serve a full term in 1948.

7. Under Roosevelt and Truman, Democrats held control of the national administration for an unprecedented and uninterrupted 20 years.

E. Era of Stalemate

1. Republicans returned to the White House in 1953 after they elected Dwight D. Eisenhower, popular general of World War II.

      a. Republicans also won control of both houses of Congress in 1952, but lost both houses in the 1954, 1956, and 1958 elections.

      b. Twenty-second amendment barred Republicans from running Eisenhower for third term after he was reelected in 1956.

2. Eisenhower's Vice President, Richard M. Nixon, was nominated by Republicans to oppose Democratic Senator John F. Kennedy in 1960 presidential contest.

      a. Kennedy and vice presidential running mate, Senator Lyndon B. Johnson, won in a close popular-vote count.

      b. Kennedy carried 23 states; Nixon carried 26, but Kennedy received 303 electoral votes to 219 for Nixon.

      c. Democrats retained control of both houses of Congress in 1960.

      d. Election of 1960 was followed by split in Republican party between liberals and conservatives.

3. Following assassination of President Kennedy in 1963, Vice President Lyndon B. Johnson assumed presidency.

4. Presidential election of 1964 was unprecedented landslide for Democrats.

      a. Senator Barry Goldwater's nomination by Republicans marked a victory for the conservative wing of the party.

      b. President Johnson's record victory in the presidential contest helped elect one of the strongest Democratic congressional majorities in history.

      c. Aside from his notable breakthrough in the South, Goldwater carried only his home state, Arizona.

      d. Election results interpreted as new proof that only a moderate candidate can be elected President.

II. THE TWO-PARTY SYSTEM

A. Traditional in American Politics

1. During most of history, power has alternated between two major parties.
2. Minor parties do arise and influence national politics.
3. No minor party has ever elected a President.
4. Major parties sometimes disappear, but development of new second party is traditional pattern.
5. Minor parties sometimes elect congressmen.
6. Minor parties have occasionally dominated state and local politics.
7. One of major parties may dominate national politics for lengthy period, but resurgence of second party is pattern.
8. Most voters consistently identify with one of two major parties.

B. Historical Notes

1. Political parties unmentioned in U.S. Constitution.
2. To Founding Fathers, parties represented factions, and factions were to be avoided.
3. Yet, the Constitution made no provision for nomination of presidential candidates, which came to be an essential function of the parties.
4. Parties are so basic to the American political system as to be considered an unwritten part of the Constitution.

C. Advantages of a Two-Party System

1. Voters can be confronted with an either-or choice, thus simplifying decisions and political processes.

2. Electoral decisions are usually majority decisions, encouraging majority support for governmental policies.

3. Governmental stability is enhanced by a two-party system which is lacking in a multi-party system.

D. Influences for Persistence of Two-Party System

1. Ratification of the Constitution confronted the nation with a yea-or-nay decision, and political questions have tended to take the same form ever since.

2. Winner-take-all nature of the Electoral College discourages growth of third parties.

3. One-member congressional districts—as compared with a system of proportional representation—makes it difficult for third parties to win representation in Congress.

4. Great ideological split of the Civil War tended to encourage either-or nature of American political decisions.

5. Constitutional separation of church and state discourages formation of church-based parties.

6. Lack of strong class-consciousness has discouraged formation of parties on class basis.

7. Political dualism.

   a. Enables members of one political party to find unity in agreement on basic principles, while disagreeing on many less-basic principles.

   b. Facilitates a spectrum of ideological views within each of major parties.

   c. Discourages formation of dissident splinter groups by making it easy for them to find place in one of major parties.

E. Status of Third Parties

1. With varying force, have arisen periodically throughout American history.

2. Commonly arise as one-issue parties directed toward one particular reform (such as prohibition or monetary reform).

3. Seldom successful in national elections.

4. Have proved useful as "trial balloons" to test popularity of proposed reform.

5. Major importance rests in influencing major parties to adopt third-party proposals which demonstrate broad support.

6. Once the issue has been adopted by major party, third parties have little reason or will for survival.

III. PARTY ORGANIZATION

A. General Characteristics

1. Resembles federal structure, with organization surrounding candidates at each electoral level, national, state, district, and local.

2. Resemble loose associations of state and local units.

3. Little chance for discipline is reflected in national party organization.

4. Party strength is often said to originate at the bottom, or precinct level, and flow to the top.

B. National Parties

1. Highest authority in both major parties is the national convention.

   a. Meets every four years.

   b. Convention represents states and territories according to formula adopted by party.

   c. Four convention functions.

     (1) Nominate party's candidates for President and Vice President.

(2) Adopt party's national platform.

(3) Adopt rules of the party.

(4) Elect the national committee—which selects the time and place for the next national convention and may exercise limited executive direction until next convention.

    (a) Committeemen are formally elected by national party conventions.

    (b) In fact, committeemen are named by state party conventions or committees, or else elected in state party primaries.

2. National chairman.

  a. Manages presidential campaign.

  b. Is formally elected by national committee.

  c. Is actually named by party's presidential nominee at close of convention.

  d. Serves as presidential candidate's lieutenant for management of the national party.

  e. Chairman of party successful in presidential campaign may serve as dispenser of patronage for President and may be appointed himself to Cabinet position.

3. Congressional campaign committees.

  a. Appointed by party caucuses in House and Senate, respectively.

  b. Members are commonly Senators not up for reelection or House members without strong opposition for reelection.

  c. Responsible for helping with money, speakers, and other aids for party nominees, especially in doubtful districts.

  d. Committee's activities especially important in off-year congressional elections, when there is no presidential candidate to spearhead party's efforts.

  e. Effectiveness weakened by lack of control over who are to run as party's nominees.

C. Organization at State and Local Levels

1. State hierarchy.

  a. State committee.

    (1) Members chosen at county or district level.

    (2) Have narrowly limited power.

    (3) Members often dominated by incumbent officeholders.

  b. State chairman.

    (1) Often chosen by governor or U.S. senator.

    (2) Power varies greatly according to state and circumstance, but may become powerful enough to dictate party's gubernatorial nominee.

D. The "Grass Roots"

1. Below the state level, party structure consists of a maze of numerous county and district committees, organized around elective offices at whatever level of government.

2. Some county, district, and local committees may exist only on paper, not at all in fact.

3. When they do actually exist, county, district, and local committees vary widely in degree of activity, are often small and poorly organized.

4. In some states, effectiveness of local party organizations is highly dependent on patronage.

IV. THE ONE-PARTY PHENOMENON IN AMERICA

A. General Characteristics

1. Both major parties and some minor parties offer candidates for national office and campaign on national issues in all 50 states.

2. Historical voting patterns which have reflected dominance by one party in a state have led to its being labeled a "one party state."
   a. States of the Deep South remained solidly Democratic for many decades after the Civil War.
   b. New England and, until the 1930s, mid-Atlantic states have been dependable Republican strongholds.
   c. In one-party states, factions develop within the broad ideological spectrum of a single party, sometimes resembling two-party rivalry.

B. The Trend in One-Party States

1. In the past five decades, two-party competition has developed within most states, so that to-day there are fewer one-party states than at any time since 1865.
   a. Once-firm Democratic dominance in the "solid South" has been shaken in recent national elections.
   b. Once considered a firm fortress of Republicanism, Maine has recently elected a Democratic governor and U.S. senator, gave its electoral vote to the Democratic presidential candidate in 1968.

C. The Rural-Urban Cleavage

1. Great urban centers of industrial states, like New York City and Chicago, are commonly considered "safe" for Democratic candidates for national office.
2. Rural votes in industrial states like New York and Illinois are commonly expected to be predominantly Republican in national elections.

SELECTED TEST QUESTIONS

I. Multiple Choice

1. The first U.S. political party to support a strong national government was the:
   (a) Federalist party; (b) anti-Federalist party; (c) Whig party; (d) Republican party.
2. In 1800 the Republican party was swept into office under the leadership of:
   (a) Alexander Hamilton; (b) Thomas Jefferson; (c) John Adams; (d) Andrew Jackson.
3. The Democratic party won an unprecedented landslide victory in 1964 with the presidential candidacy of:
   (a) John F. Kennedy; (b) Barry Goldwater; (c) Lyndon B. Johnson; (d) Hubert Humphrey.
4. In 1860, the first Republican presidential victory elected:
   (a) William Seward; (b) Grover Cleveland; (c) William McKinley; (d) Abraham Lincoln.
5. After the Civil War, the party which became identified with low tariffs and states' rights was:
   (a) the Republican party; (b) the Whig party; (c) the Democratic party; (d) the Progressive party.

II. True-False

1. The major significance of third parties in the United States has been their role as "trial balloons" to test the popularity of policy proposals.
2. The electoral college system and single-member congressional districts serve to discourage third parties.
3. No third-party movement has ever succeeded in electing a President or congressman.
4. After presidential elections, the national chairman of the successful party has frequently been appointed to the Cabinet.
5. With the election of President John F. Kennedy in 1960, the Democratic party lost control of both houses of Congress.

CHAPTER 14

Elections

INTRODUCTION

"Vote! Vote! Regardless of how you vote, get out and vote!" All mature Americans are accustomed to being besieged by such pleas. And convincing statistics are advanced which indicate that a smaller proportion of Americans vote than citizens of most European countries. And yet, voting remains a considerable chore in most states.

Laws controlling the conduct of elections vary widely from one state to another. While encouraging citizens to register and vote, many states have erected formidable barriers to effective voting in the form of difficult registration procedures, incomprehensible long ballots, and through other technical requirements.

The U.S. Census Bureau has estimated that Americans are confronted with more than 100,000 elections each year, considering all offices within the 50 states. Within the outlines of the United States Constitution, state legislatures are responsible for setting the ground rules regulating the electoral process. States must comply with the fifteenth amendment's enfranchisement of blacks, the nineteenth amendment's enfranchisement of women, the twenty-sixth amendment's enfranchisement of eighteen-year-olds, and federal statutes relating to voting and elections. Otherwise the prerogative remains with state legislatures.

Some discriminatory state barriers to voting, such as the poll tax and literacy tests, have been ruled out by the national government. In addition, recent federal court decisions indicate that lengthy residence requirements for voter registration are on the way out.

Many states undoubtedly have encouraged citizens to vote while at the same time erecting arbitrary barriers to equitable exercise of the franchise. Effective action to expand voter eligibility has come from the national government with some degree of consistency in recent decades.

I. THE VOTING PREROGATIVE

A. Registration

1. Most states require registration as a precondition to voting.
2. Registration requires appearance before an election registrar during a fixed period before the election.
3. Typical registration requirements.
   a. Twenty-one years of age (suspended by ratification of twenty-sixth amendment).
   b. American citizen.
   c. Term of residence in state, commonly one year.
   d. Term of residence in county, commonly six months.
   e. Term of residence in precinct, commonly thirty days.
   f. Laws of several states require a shorter term of residence for participation in presidential elections.
4. Reasons for registration requirements.
   a. To compel the prospective voter to orient himself to state and local conditions before he votes.
   b. To prevent vote fraud growing out of multiple voting.

    5. Abuses of registration.
        a. In a society as highly mobile as that of the United States, the one-year residence require-
           ment disfranchises many otherwise qualified voters.
        b. Discriminatory registration laws and practices have often been used to deny the ballot to
           blacks, college students, migrant workers, and ethnic minorities.
    6. Types of registration.
        a. Permanent.
            (1) In many states, the voter remains registered unless he moves to another election district.
            (2) In some states, the voter must re-register if he fails to vote in two successive elections.
            (3) Difficult to administer.
        b. Periodic.
            (1) Voter must re-register before each election or at fixed intervals.
            (2) Inconvenient to voter and reduces election turnout.
            (3) Keeps poll list up to date.
            (4) Easy to administer.
        c. Absentee.
            (1) For voters who must be absent from state during registration period.
            (2) Voter is commonly expected to return to permanent residence in his voting district.

B. Primary Elections

    1. Party primary is method used in almost all states for choosing party candidates for congres-
       sional, state, and local offices.
    2. Major parties have separate primaries in most states.
    3. Presidential nominees are selected by party convention, rather than by party primary election.
    4. Financed by the public treasury.
    5. Since it is easy to qualify as a candidate in a party primary, voters may be confronted with a
       long list of names.
    6. In a *closed primary,* voters must acknowledge membership in the party before being allowed
       to vote.
    7. Any qualified voter, regardless of party affiliation, may vote in an *open primary.*
    8. Under the *convention-primary* system, one primary candidate for the party's nomination
       carries the endorsement of the party's convention.
    9. Some states use the *runoff primary,* matching the two top-running candidates after a primary
       in which no one man received a majority of the votes.
   10. In *nonpartisan* primary, candidates run without party designation; two candidates receiving
       the most votes oppose each other in a general election.

C. Voting

    1. The Australian ballot system, used in the United States, is widely accepted as a model for
       fair elections.
        a. Government prints uniform ballots.
        b. Secrecy of ballot is assured.
    2. The *long ballot,* listing literally hundreds of names of candidates for major and minor offices
       is used in most states.
        a. The long ballot is often criticized for expecting voters to indicate preferences on matters
           in which they cannot be well informed.
        b. Another criticism is that the long ballot reflects a disintegrated structure in public ad-
           ministration, in which minor officeholders are elected who might better be appointed by an
           executive official.

    c. Origin of the long ballot is usually traced to the era of Jacksonian Democracy, in the mid-nineteenth century.

    d. Continued use of the long ballot is said to reflect the average citizen's faith in the electoral process as an essential element of democracy and a faith in the virtue of popularly reached decisions.

    e. The more obscure the office to be filled, the fewer will be the number of votes cast for candidates.

  3. "Short-ballot" reform advocates have had limited success.

II. ELECTION FINANCING

A. Cost of Campaigns

1. Campaign financing is a subject not well understood by most voters.
2. National campaigns are especially expensive.
    a. Three top parties spent an estimated $50 million in the 1968 presidential campaign.
    b. Efforts to restrict expenditures have had little effect.
3. Much money spent on national, state, and local elections is unreported.
4. In a large state, even a statewide campaign may cost more than a million dollars.
5. Excessive length of U.S. election campaigns forces costs up.

B. Source of Campaign Finances

1. Although government financing of campaigns has been recommended in the United States, as is the practice in England, the proposal has made little headway.
2. Many candidates dip into own pockets, especially in primary campaigns.
3. Personal friends of candidates sometimes help.
4. Sympathetic interest groups often help with various kinds of donations.
5. Party treasuries are major source of money to finance general election campaigns, as distinguished from primaries.

C. Sources of National Party Finances

1. Fewer than 10 percent of voters contribute to either parties or candidates.
2. Business and industrial executives commonly contribute to parties—especially the Republican party.
3. Parties sponsor various fund-raising events.

D. Financing the Local Parties

1. Large part of the money comes from officeholders and candidates.
2. Government employees are sometimes assessed a fixed percentage of earnings—a practice widely held in disrepute.
3. Interest groups are often generous donors.
4. Patronage seekers often contribute.

E. Efforts by Government to Police Party Finances

1. Both national and state governments have attempted regulation with limited success.
2. Major efforts by national government to regulate party finances.
    a. *Corrupt Practices Act of 1925.*
      (1) Sought to limit expenditures in U.S. House of Representatives campaign to $2,500, in a U.S. Senate race to $10,000.

(2) Alternate limit was three cents for each vote cast for office in last general election.

b. *Hatch Act of 1939.*

(1) Limited campaign contributions.

(2) Restricted political activity by employees of federal government.

c. *Taft-Hartley Act of 1947.*

(1) Barred spending by corporations and labor unions in elections to national offices.

(2) Also applied to party primary elections for national offices.

d. *Federal Election Campaign Act of 1971.*

(1) Limits campaign expenditures for advertising in presidential and congressional campaigns.

(2) Requires full reporting of both sources and uses of campaign funds.

(3) Limits advertising expenditures to ten cents per potential voter.

III. CAMPAIGNING FOR NATIONAL OFFICE

A. Running for a U.S. House Seat

1. Background of local political experience highly desirable.

2. Acquaintance with people throughout district can help form basic campaign organization.

3. Timing is important.

a. State, local, and national political trends may be vital.

b. Presidential-election year versus off-year election poses crucial question.

c. Attractiveness of other candidates must be considered.

4. First target: the primary race.

a. Parties remain neutral in primary elections.

b. Candidate must build own personal organization.

(1) Support of party leaders can be crucial.

(2) Sympathetic interest groups can provide nucleus of organization and following.

5. Candidate must plan to divide his campaign spending between primary campaign and general election.

6. Final lap: the general election.

a. If victorious in the primary, the candidate may expect the windfall of formal support from the party.

b. As the party's nominee, the candidate gains increased exposure — especially in the press and in party circles.

c. Personal contacts, so essential in the primary, remain important in the general election.

B. The Campaign for U.S. Senate

1. Since election to the Senate requires a statewide race, the best steppingstone is often said to be a state office filled by statewide election, such as governorship or attorney generalship.

2. However, many House members have succeeded in Senate races.

3. Six-year term makes office exceptionally attractive.

4. Senators receive much greater national publicity than House members, and candidates receive greater publicity than House candidates.

5. Cost of statewide campaign is often measured in hundreds of thousands of dollars.

6. Television has assumed a role of increasing importance in recent Senate campaigns.

IV. SEEKING THE PINNACLE—THE PRESIDENTIAL CAMPAIGN

A. Winning the Nomination

1. Both major parties select presidential candidates by means of the nominating convention.
    a. First national convention of a major party was in 1831 under leadership of President Jackson.
    b. Parties make own formulas for representation of states at national conventions.
    c. Two factors are reflected in state representation at national conventions of two major parties.
        (1) Electoral strength.
        (2) Party success in preceding election.
2. National convention delegates are chosen by a variety of methods, including state party conventions and state presidential primaries.
3. Presidential primaries.
    a. Attract relatively low voter participation.
    b. Broadly viewed as popularity contests only.
    c. Some candidates ignore them.
4. Much criticism is directed at the presidential nominating convention.
5. Many proposals have been advanced for presidential nominating national primaries.

B. The General Election Campaign

1. Technically, the President will be elected, not by the popular vote, but by the vote of *presidential electors.*
2. Each state has as many electoral votes as it has members in the U.S. House of Representatives, plus two—a total of 535 in the nation.
3. The candidate who gets most votes in any state receives *all* of that state's electoral votes.
4. The grueling campaign.
    a. Major task is keeping 50 state parties in line and active.
    b. Interest-group appeal must be planned and pursued with care.
    c. Candidates must travel extensively, gaining in-person exposure.
    d. Large population states, with large electoral votes, have priority for attention.

V. PRESIDENT MAKERS: THE ELECTORAL COLLEGE

A. What Is the Electoral College?

1. Provided by the Constitution as indirect method of electing the President.
2. A reflection of the pre-Constitution sovereignty of the states, the provision allows each state the number of electoral votes that it has members of the U.S. House of Representatives, plus two—for a total of 535 votes in the Electoral College.
3. In some states, voters actually vote for a slate of electors, rather than for presidential nominees.
    a. All electors of each state are bound by tradition—and in 15 states by law—to cast votes for presidential nominee who received most popular votes in their respective states.
    b. Electors have occasionally abandoned custom and cast ballots for personal preferences.

B. Criticism of the Electoral College

1. It was designed for a day when limitations on transportation and communication made it impossible for all voters to learn qualifications of presidential candidates in order to vote intelligently.
2. Improvements in transportation and communication have brought the presidential candidate much closer to the voter, often into his living room through the medium of television, thus eliminating the need for indirect election of a President by "men of affairs."

3. By its very nature, and by the independent status of the electors, the Electoral College poses the possibility of a small group of electors joining in collusion to thwart the will of the people.
4. In short, the Electoral College system does not guarantee that the popular choice will become President.
5. Since voting strength of the states is not based on population alone, it is often charged that the Electoral College gives small-population states disproportionate strength in electing a President.
6. On the other hand, since it is so important for presidential candidates to win the electoral vote in large-population states, they are often charged with giving inadequate campaign attention to small-population states.

C. Presidential-Election Reform Proposals

1. Scrap the Electoral College, by constitutional amendment, and base the presidential election on the nationwide popular vote.
2. Abolish the electors, but retain the present weighted-voting formula, so that a state's electoral vote would automatically go to the candidate receiving the most votes in each state.
3. Grant each candidate a proportion of the electoral vote in each state reflecting the proportion of popular votes he received (the Lodge-Gossett proposal).

SELECTED TEST QUESTIONS

I. Multiple Choice

1. The most consistent vigil over voting rights has been maintained by the:
   (a) national government; (b) state governments; (c) county governments; (d) city governments.
2. The term of residence required for registering to vote in many states has been:
   (a) one month; (b) one year; (c) five years; (d) ten years.
3. Expenditures of the three top parties in the 1968 presidential campaign are estimated at:
   (a) $1 million; (b) $10 million; (c) $50 million; (d) $70 million.
4. The number of voters who contribute money to either parties or candidates is:
   (a) 5-10 percent; (b) 20 percent; (c) 25 percent; (d) 50 percent.
5. A limit on advertising expenditures of ten cents per potential voter was prescribed by:
   (a) the Corrupt Practices Act of 1925; (b) the Hatch Act of 1939; (c) the Taft-Hartley Act of 1947; the Federal Election Campaign Act of 1971.

II. True-False

1. Efforts to limit or publicize campaign spending have proved generally ineffective.
2. The Taft-Hartley Act of 1947 barred all corporations and labor organizations from spending money in national elections.
3. The use of professional campaign managers in recent election campaigns has reduced the cost of seeking office.
4. Voter registration laws have increased the turnout of voters in state and national elections.
5. The long ballot is considered a major deterrent to voter turnout.

CHAPTER 15

The Organization of Congress

INTRODUCTION

Article I of the United States Constitution creates a *bicameral* (two-house) national legislature which is called the Congress of the United States. The two house are called the United States Senate and the United States House of Representatives. All legislative powers of the national government were given to the Congress.

Article I is the longest and most detailed of the seven articles written by the men who created the Constitution. Why so much detail in this article? Probably because the men who wrote the Constitution were familiar with legislatures. They had served in their state legislatures and were aware of legislative problems and needs. They had had little experience with the executive branch of government—and, indeed, had some inclination to view executive power with suspicion. Under the Articles of Confederation, the Congress of the Confederation had been the only agency of government. The men who wrote the Constitution saw in the granting of additional powers to the Congress the greatest opportunity for remedying the weaknesses of the Confederation.

The Congress of the Confederation had been a *unicameral* (one-house) legislative body. Why, then, was the unicameral feature abandoned and a bicameral Congress created in its place? This question reflects one of the greatest disagreements confronted by the convention in the summer of 1787. Large-population states insisted on representation based on population in the new Congress. Small-population states, on the other hand, wanted to continue the practice of the Congress of the Confederation—the principle of equal representation for each state, regardless of population. It was in the face of this impasse over representation that George Washington, Chairman of the Convention, is said to have written a friend that it was foredoomed to failure and expressing regret that he had ever become involved with it.

This darkest moment of the Philadelphia convention was brightened by introduction and adoption of the Connecticut Compromise, also called the "Great Compromise," which resolved the question of representation in the new Congress. Under the terms of this agreement, a two-house legislature was created—with equal representation for each state in the "upper" house, or Senate, and representation based on population in the "lower" house, or House of Representatives.

The Connecticut Compromise is said to have been the "price of union." This compromise pleased the small states and made it possible for them to agree to the establishment of a strong central government.

Although a bicameral national legislature grew out of a compromise and was necessary to break the constitutional deadlock of 1787, it has attracted an increasing volume of criticism in recent years. Equal representation of states in the United States Senate has given a disproportionate influence to sparsely settled states. Although the states are represented by population in the House of Representatives, bills must win approval in both houses before they become law. So the outcome of the Great Compromise of 1787 is reflected in the daily activities of Congress even today.

I. REPRESENTATION IN CONGRESS

A. The House—Representation by Districts

1. Representation intended to reflect shifts in population.
2. Except for 1842 and 1920, House membership has been adjusted after every census to make representation conform to population among the states.

3. Membership of House was frozen at 435 in 1929 and automatic plan was adopted for assigning membership to states after every U.S. census.
4. Since 1929, Florida, California, Oregon, and Washington have steadily gained population and House seats at the expense of other states.
5. Each state is entitled to at least one representative.
6. In 1842 Congress required every state with more than one representative to designate districts from which individual congressmen would be elected.
7. Single-member system assures representation to wide variety of population segments and interest groups, strengthening the representative character of the House.
8. State legislatures responsible for creating congressional districts.
9. Partisan interests of state legislators sometimes causes them to *gerrymander*—that is, draw congressional districts for partisan political advantage.
10. U.S. Supreme Court has ruled that districts must be as nearly equal in population as is practicable.
11. Cities have steadily gained population, with a resulting gain in representation at the expense of rural representation.

B. The Senate—Equal Representation for the States

1. Constitution provides that each state, regardless of its population, is entitled to two senators.
2. Until 1913 and ratification of the seventeenth amendment, senators were elected by state legislatures, since that time have been popularly elected.
3. Reflecting the undemocratic nature of Senate representation, about 20 percent of population elects a majority of the senators.

II. THE MEMBERS OF CONGRESS

A. Qualifications for Membership

1. House membership requirements.
   a. Twenty-five years of age.
   b. U.S. citizen seven years.
   c. When elected, inhabitant of state in which chosen.
2. Senate membership requirements.
   a. Thirty years of age.
   b. U.S. citizen nine years.
   c. When elected, inhabitant of state in which chosen.

B. Selection of Members

1. Prior to ratification of seventeenth amendment in 1913, House members were elected by people, and senators were elected by state legislatures.
2. Since ratification of seventeenth amendment, House members have been chosen in district-wide popular elections, senators in statewide elections.
3. Methods of electing senators and representatives is regulated largely by state law, with detailed variations among the states.
4. Nomination of candidates is most commonly by direct party primary.
5. Election of representatives from single-member districts by secret ballot is required by national law.
6. Congress has also placed legal limits on campaign expenditures, but enforcement has proved difficult.

7. Popular election of senators was expected to deemphasize the importance of money in becoming a senator, but this hope has not been realized.
8. Several proposals have been made for extending length of congressional terms.

C. Who Are the Lawmakers?

1. Well above average American in education, age, and financial means.
2. Characteristics of members of ninetieth Congress.
   a. Average age of representatives was fifty-one, of senators, fifty-eight.
   b. Most were long residents of districts and states they represented.
   c. Affiliation with major religious faith matched cross-section of population.
   d. Eighty-eight percent had attended college or professional school.
   e. Commonly had previous political experience in state and local government.
   f. Majority were lawyers.
   g. Twelve women and seven blacks in membership.
   h. Economically and socially, upper-middle class predominated.

III. PARTIES AND LEADERSHIP IN CONGRESS

A. Role of Parties

1. Political party influence in Congress sometimes called "invisible government" of Congress.
2. Parties control the structure of leadership.
3. Two major parties predominate.
4. Party loyalty required for individual advancement in Congress.

B. Party Caucuses or Conferences

1. Each major party has a caucus (or conference, as the Republicans call theirs) in each house of Congress.
2. A caucus consists of all members of one of the major parties in one house of Congress.
3. The caucus serves as the instrument of party government and discipline within its respective house of Congress. Before Congress meets, the party caucuses elect party officers for their respective houses of Congress and name candidates, for key legislative posts, such as Speaker of the House.
4. Caucuses rarely meet after the original organizational meeting prior to each session of Congress.
5. Caucus may take a party stand on pending legislation.

C. Organs of the Caucus

1. Policy committee.
   a. Manages party's legislative program.
   b. Membership designed to represent various sections of country.
2. Floor leaders.
   a. One is named by each of major party caucuses in each house.
   b. Direct their respective party's legislative programs in the two houses.
   c. Manage legislative strategy in pursuit of party policy.
   d. After the Speaker, the House majority party leader is considered number two man in promotion of his party's legislative program.
   e. Assistant floor leaders, or "whips," are selected by the caucus to assist the floor leaders and canvass views of party members on pending legislation.

D. Speaker of the House

1. Most powerful member of Congress.
2. Always member of majority party in House.
3. Elected by House following nomination by majority party caucus.
4. Presides over House sessions.
5. Prior to 1910, appointed members to standing committees in House.
6. Prior to 1910, served as chairman of Rules Committee, most powerful committee in the House.
7. Appoints all special, select, and conference committees.
8. Entitled to vote on all measures before the House.
9. Uses his influence to aid party's program.
10. Rules on parliamentary procedure.

E. Officers of the Senate

1. More individualistic Senate has no officer with powers comparable to powers of the Speaker of the House.
2. Presiding officer is the Vice President, who is not elected by the Senate and so may not necessarily belong to majority party in the Senate.
   a. Vice President is always of President's political party, thus in position to represent President before the Senate.
   b. Vice President may vote on Senate business only to break a tie vote by Senators.
3. President *pro tempore* (pro tem) is elected by the Senate from its membership to share the presiding functions with the Vice President.
   a. Often more influential than the Vice President, because he is a member of the Senate.
   b. Always a member of the majority party, unlike the Vice President.

IV. THE POWERFUL STANDING COMMITTEES OF CONGRESS

A. Advantages of the Committee System

1. Makes possible more careful review of proposed legislation.
2. Saves time of congressmen by referring most matters to committee for study and recommendation.
3. Allows congressmen to specialize in subject matter of committee(s) to which they belong.

B. Number of Committees

1. The House has 20 standing committees and the Senate has 16.
2. Natural tendency for number of committees to increase must be occasionally countered by trimming back and consolidating committees.

C. Importance of Committees in Congress

1. In the U.S. Congress, committees play a more powerful role in shaping the legislative output than in any other deliberative body in the world.
2. Because of the large number of House members, the House must rely more heavily on committees than the individualistic Senate.
3. Individual congressmen are especially eager for appointment to committee pertinent to his constituents.
4. Committee appointment is important enough to have major bearing on the political and legislative success of individual congressmen.

D. Membership on Standing Committees

1. On all but a few committees (Appropriations, Ways and Means, House Rules) membership is divided between the two major parties to reflect proportion of membership in each house.
2. With some exceptions, each House member serves on one standing committee, each senator on one.
3. Committee appointments for new members of Congress are made by committee on committees, an organ of the caucus, and ratified by the respective houses.

E. Chairmanships and Seniority

1. Committee chairman has great power over his committee and proposed legislation referred to it.
2. The formula of *seniority* has evolved as method of determining chairmanships by computing the number of years of continuous service on the committee by each committee member.
3. Chairman is member of majority party with most years of continuous service on the committee.

F. Criticisms of Seniority System

1. It enhances the power of committee members from one-party states, where congressmen are traditionally returned to office without general-election competition.
2. No demonstrable relationship between seniority and ability.
3. Entrenches conservatism.

V. OTHER COMMITTEES

A. Committee of the Whole

1. Used only by the House.
2. Temporary chairman appointed by the Speaker.
3. Rules are suspended for less formal proceedings in consideration of matters of general national interest.

B. Special and Select Committees

1. At one time were responsible for many investigations.
2. Sometimes made up of members of House and Senate to form *joint committee.*
3. Often handed tasks which cannot be carried out well by standing committees.
4. Established for limited time and limited purpose.

C. Conference Committees

1. Joint committees composed of members of both houses.
2. Appointed to iron out differences in House and Senate versions of a bill after it has passed both houses.

D. The Powerful House Rules Committee

1. Often called the most powerful committee in Congress.
2. Serves as "traffic cop" in legislative process of the House.
3. Must approve every important piece of legislation which goes to House floor for a vote.
4. Decides how much time may be spent in debate on any measure, conditions under which it will be referred to the House.
5. May approve a bill, kill it, rewrite it, or send it back to committee for revision.
6. Most important function is eliminating unimportant measures from congressional overload and expediting important proposals.
7. No counterpart in the Senate.

SELECTED TEST QUESTIONS

I. Multiple Choice

1. Congress was created as a *bicameral* legislature because:
   (a) it is the most efficient form; (b) two houses were thought necessary for such a vast nation; (c) a compromise was needed in a dispute over the basis of representation; (d) the Congress of the Confederation had been bicameral.
2. The bicameral national legislature grew out of:
   (a) the Virginia Plan; (b) the New Jersey Plan; (c) the Rhode Island Plan; (d) the Connecticut Compromise.
3. Probably the most powerful man in Congress is:
   (a) the Speaker of the House; (b) the president *pro tempore* of the Senate; (c) the Vice President; (d) chairman of the Senate rules committee.
4. Probably the most powerful committee in Congress is the:
   (a) Senate Rules Committee; (b) House Rules Committee; (c) Senate Committee on Committees; (d) House Committee on Committees.
5. A committee of House and Senate members, assigned to iron out differences between the House and Senate versions of a measure which has passed both houses is called a:
   (a) conference committee; (b) standing committee; (c) select committee; (d) committee of the whole.

II. True-False

1. The seniority system in the committees of Congress is generally thought to place power in the hands of the most competent.
2. The leadership in the House is generally considered more powerful than the leadership in the Senate.
3. Although the Vice President may preside over the Senate, his powers are not as great as those of the Speaker of the House.
4. The seniority system in Congress favors congressmen from two-party states.
5. Congressmen tend to show little interest in their standing committee assignments.

CHAPTER 16

Congress at Work

INTRODUCTION

The Constitution vests *all* the legislative power of the national government in the Congress. However, under the American system of federalism, the legislative powers of Congress are restricted to a relatively narrow area of legitimate interest. Congress has only those powers delegated to it by the Constitution. The delegation of legislative powers to Congress is found in Article I, Section 8, where these powers are enumerated. Hence delegated powers are sometimes called enumerated powers. Whichever they are called, they are vested in the Congress of the United States. Powers not delegated remained with the states, as specifically provided by the tenth amendment.

Three powers granted to Congress have proved to be much broader in practice than they would appear on the face of Article I. These three have brought with them many other powers which may or may not have been intended for the national government by a majority of the men who framed the Constitution. These are the commerce power, the taxing power, and the war power. In its exercise of these powers, Congress has succeeded in acquiring broad powers of regulation.

For example, the taxing power may have been granted Congress for revenue purposes, but by its selective levying of taxes, Congress has been able to discourage or eliminate practices it has considered harmful to the welfare of the nation.

Through its authority to regulate interstate commerce, Congress has found it possible to establish a nationwide police force, which certainly was not foreseen by the authors of the Constitution, and to regulate employment and manufacturing in all parts of the nation. Through its war power, shared with the President, Congress has found it possible to do almost anything it wishes during time of war which will contribute to a victory.

I. KINDS OF CONGRESSIONAL ACTION

A. Bills

1. Method of enacting general legislation.
2. Become *laws* when they receive majority vote in both houses of Congress and signature of President.
3. *Private bill* is one intended to benefit an individual.
4. *Public bill* is general legislation dealing with classes of individuals.

B. Joint Resolutions

1. Similar to bills.
2. Become laws when passed by majority in both houses and signed by President.
3. May be used for proposing constitutional amendments, in which case signature of President is unnecessary.
4. May be used to express congressional approval of executive action—especially in matters of foreign policy.
5. Have been used for ratification of treaties to circumvent the two-thirds vote requirement in the Senate for treaty ratification.

C. Concurrent Resolutions

1. Not submitted to the President.
2. Intended to express attitudes on which both houses are agreed.
3. Have no actual force outside Congress.
4. One use is for creation of joint congressional committees.

D. Simple Resolutions

1. Deal with affairs of one house only.
2. Serve to express attitudes of one house of Congress.
3. Do not require signature of President.
4. Do not have force of law.
5. Usually employed for making or amending rules of procedure in one house or for advising President on matters of executive responsibility.

E. Orders

1, Not submitted to President.
2. Commands or requests of one house, usually on procedural matters.

II. KINDS OF LAWS

A. New Law

1. Often marks new policy direction by Congress.
2. Usually attracts much publicity.

B. Amendments to Existing Law

1. May supplement, clarify, consolidate, or repeal existing legislation.
2. Often in form of remedial amendments to achieve original intent of Congress.

C. Appropriation Acts

1. Required to provide the money necessary for running government.
2. All expenditures must be authorized by Congress, thus giving the legislative branch "power of the purse."
3. By custom, appropriations originate in the House.
4. By their provisions, appropriation acts often give direction to governmental administration.

III. LEGISLATIVE POWERS OF CONGRESS

A. Delegated Powers

1. Also called *"enumerated powers."*
2. Are listed or enumerated in Article I, Section 8, of U.S. Constitution.
3. Eighteen powers are enumerated.

B. Implied Powers

1. Powers which are implied by the delegated powers.
2. Based on "necessary and proper" clause—Article I, Section 8, Paragraph 18.
3. First declared by the U.S. Supreme Court in case of *McCulloch v. Maryland* (1819).

C. Inherent Powers

1. Powers which belong to a sovereign state simply because it is a sovereign state.
2. Commonly apply to external or international matters.
3. Example of inherent power of national government is power of exploration, discovery, and accession of territory, although the Constitution is silent on the subject.
4. Need not be stated in the Constitution or elsewhere.

D. Reserved Powers

1. Powers not given to Congress by the Constitution, therefore denied to the national government.
2. Powers *reserved* to the states expressly by the tenth amendment.
3. Commonest example is the *police power*—the power of states to regulate the behavior of persons within their respective borders.

E. Concurrent Powers

1. Powers exercised by both the states and the national government.
2. Most obvious example is power to tax.

F. Prohibited Powers

1. Powers denied to both state and national government, or denied to either the state or national government.
2. Commonest examples lie in area of civil liberties.

IV. NON-LEGISLATIVE POWERS OF CONGRESS

A. Constituent

1. Relates to congressional role in changing the Constitution.
2. Includes authority to propose amendments by concurrence of two-thirds of members of both houses.
3. Congress has power to determine how proposed amendments will be ratified—whether by state legislatures or by special ratifying conventions.
4. Congress may summon constitutional convention when petitioned to do so by two-thirds of the states.

B. Electoral

1. Relates to formal role played by Congress in election of President and Vice President.
2. Electoral votes are formally counted in presence of both houses.
3. In event of tie vote, election of President devolves on the House, and election of Vice President falls to the Senate.
4. If electoral votes are contested, Congress must settle the dispute.

C. Executive Powers

1. Includes power of Congress to appoint its own committees.
2. Senate exercises executive power when it confirms presidential appointments and gives advice and consent to the ratification of treaties.

D. Directory and Supervisory Powers

1. Relates to control of Congress over executive establishment.
2. President is dependent on Congress to create and finance administrative agencies.

3. Congress prescribes the roles of administrative agencies.
4. Congress constantly reviews the work of administrative agencies.
   a. Most agencies must report annually to Congress.
   b. Personal contacts by congressmen in quest of information and explanations.
   c. Committees often review agency operation.
   d. Agency review is common when administrators undertake to justify budget requests.

E. Inquisitorial Power

1. Congressional authority to conduct investigations.
2. Congress may investigate into any field in which it has authority to legislate.
3. Investigations may be conducted by entire Senate or House — or, more commonly, by standing or special committees.
4. Congress may subpoena witnesses and evidence.

F. Judicial Powers

1. Each house is authorized by the Constitution to judge the qualifications of its own members.
2. The power to impeach civil officers of the national government is vested in the House of Representatives.
   a. Impeachment may be voted by a simple majority in the House of Representatives, but impeachment amounts only to a formal charge, which must be heard and ruled on by the Senate.
   b. Military officers and congressmen not subject to impeachment.
   c. Committee appointed by House is responsible for pressing impeachment charges in trial before the Senate.
   d. Grounds for impeachment are restricted to grave criminal offenses.
   e. Impeachment charges have been approved by the House only 12 times.
3. Power to try officials impeached by the House is vested in the Senate, sitting as a court.
   a. Chief Justice presides over trial of an impeached President.
   b. Two-thirds vote is required for conviction.
   c. Penalty is limited to removal from office and disqualification for public office.
   d. Four convictions have been voted by the Senate.
   e. Only one President, Andrew Johnson, has been impeached, and he escaped conviction by a single vote.

V. BILLS IN CONGRESS

A. Origin

1. Congressmen.
2. Administration.
3. Interest groups.

B. Introduction

1. Generally, bills may originate in either house.
2. Revenue (tax) measures must originate in the House.
3. More than 20,000 bills and resolutions are introduced in each session.
4. Between 1,000 and 1,500 measures are enacted in some form in each session.

C. Legislative Route

1. Upon introduction, each bill is numbered.
2. Presiding officer is responsible for assignment of bill to one of standing committees.

3. Committees have broad powers over legislation referred to them.
4. Proposed legislation is often assigned by committee to subcommittee for study.
5. If appropriate, public hearings may be held.
6. Pertinent information is gathered.
   a. By staff research.
   b. From lobbyists.
   c. From administrative agencies.
   d. Opinions of experts.
   e. Constituent attitudes.
7. Three possible courses of action by committee.
   a. Kill the bill.
   b. Amend the bill and report it out favorably.
   c. Report it out favorably as it was submitted.
8. If committee refuses to report bill back to its house, a *discharge petition* may be used to force the bill out of committee.
   a. Discharge petitions are rarely used.
   b. May apply after committee has had 30 days to consider bill.
   c. Petition must bear endorsement by majority of members.

D. Procedures in the House of Representatives

1. When bill is reported out of committee, it commonly goes on one of three House calendars.
   a. Union calendar.
      (1) Revenue bills.
      (2) Appropriations bills.
   b. House calendar.
      (1) Public bills.
      (2) Does not include revenue and appropriations bills.
   c. Private calendar.
   d. Bills remain on calendar for as long as two years unless acted on.
   e. Many bills die on House calendar without ever coming to vote.
   f. Revenue and taxation bills may be considered at almost any time.
   g. Bills on the House calendar must have a special order from the Rules Committee before being considered by the full House.
2. *Committee of the Whole.*
   a. Methods of dealing with much of legislative business of the House.
   b. Has advantage of informality, release from rigid House rules.
   c. Presence of 100 members constitutes quorum.
   d. Revenue and appropriations measures commonly handled by Committee of the Whole.
   e. Speakers limited to five minutes each in debate.
3. The three readings.
   a. First reading upon introduction of bill, when only the title is actually read.
   b. Second reading occurs after the bill returns from the standing committee to which it was referred, and may be an actual line-by-line reading of entire bill.
      (1) Amendments may be offered on second reading, unless banned by order of the House Rules Committee.
      (2) Second reading followed by vote on whether the bill should be printed and read a third time.
   c. Third reading is by title only, with amendments not permitted.
      (1) Debate must be on whole bill as it stands.
      (2) Vote on final passage follows third reading.

E. Procedures in the Senate

1. Bill passed by House is certified by the House Clerk and delivered to the Senate.
2. In most respects, Senate consideration of its own bills and those which originate in the House is similar to House procedures.
3. Some differences in procedures on bills reported out of committee.
   a. Senate has only two calendars.
      (1) Calendar of Business.
      (2) Executive Calendar.
   b. Senate uses Committee of the Whole only for consideration of treaties.
   c. Senate has no powerful Rules Committee, as in the House, to limit debate and bring bills to the floor.
   d. No time limits on debate in Senate.
      (1) Speakers not limited to subject pending before the Senate.
      (2) Speech or debate may be shut off only through the difficult process of *cloture* (or *closure*), which requires agreement by two-thirds of Senators.
      (3) Unlimited debate opens the door to the *filibuster*, a delaying tactic of monopolizing the floor to block Senate action.

F. Conference Committees

1. Necessary when Senate and House pass bill with differences which may result from amendment.
2. Differences must be ironed out so one bill may be sent to White House for President's signature.
3. Conference Committee compromises differences between two versions and produces one bill acceptable to both houses.
4. Most important bills must go to Conference Committee.
5. Presiding officer of each house appoints members to conference.
6. Chairman and ranking minority member from House and Senate committees which studied the bill are customarily named to Conference Committee.
7. Majority of both Senate and House groups, voting separately, must agree to compromise version.
8. Compromise legislation produced by Conference Committee may not be amended when it goes to both houses for approval.
9. Conference Committee hearings are secret and unrecorded.

VI. CONGRESSIONAL INVESTIGATIONS

A. Legitimate Purposes

1. Control over administration.
2. Discovery of areas of needed legislation.
3. Discovery of shortcomings of existing law.

B. Scope of Investigatory Power

1. All areas in which Congress has authority to legislate.
2. Although Congress has in recent decades used the power to expose and embarrass individuals, the Supreme Court has declared that such exposure must be justified in terms of the functions of Congress.
3. *House Committee on Un-American Activities* has been especially controversial in its investigations.

4. Highly publicized investigations of early 1950s encouraged abuses of individual privacy.
5. Some House Speakers have recently curbed use of mass media in investigations and hearings.

SELECTED TEST QUESTIONS

I. Multiple Choice

1. A committee of members of both houses of Congress assigned to compromise differences between House and Senate versions of a bill is called a:
   (a) Standing Committee; (b) Select Committee; (c) Conference Committee; (d) Committee of the Whole.
2. The House committee which must approve most bills which pass Congress is the:
   (a) Ways and Means Committee; (b) Rules Committee; (c) Appropriations Committee; (d) Government Operations Committee.
3. A bill may be forced out of a reluctant committee of Congress by means of a:
   (a) discharge petition; (b) cloture petition; (c) filibuster; (d) joint resolution.
4. Bills introduced in Congress are referred to standing committees by:
   (a) the Committee on Committees; (b) the presiding officer of either house; (c) the Rules Committee; (d) the majority floor leader.
5. The seldom-used method of forcing a committee to report out a bill is known as the:
   (a) discharge petition; (b) cloture petition; (c) filibuster; (d) point of order.

II. True-False

1. Congress has all those legislative powers not given by the Constitution to the states.
2. Congress has acquired broad powers of regulation from its exercise of the commerce power, taxing power, and war power.
3. In Congress, the Senate has exclusive power to originate tax legislation.
4. The powers of Congress are much narrower than the men who wrote the Constitution intended them to be.
5. At the end of the second session of each Congress, bills which have not been acted on die.

CHAPTER 17

The Presidency

INTRODUCTION

The President of the United States is the most powerful official of any democratic state in the world. He has been characterized by some writers as the most powerful official in the history of the world. And yet, the powers and prerogatives demanded of American Presidents have undoubtedly caused many of them to wring their hands in frustration, stalemated in the courses of action they deemed best for the nation and its people.

The authors of the United States Constitution were quite indefinite about what they considered to be the proper role of the President in the American government. Article II of the Constitution, which creates the presidency, is both brief and sketchy when compared with the length and detail of Article I, which created and circumscribed the legislative branch of government.

Because of the brevity of Article II, the great powers of the President of the United States grow less out of the Constitution than they do out of practice, precedent, and custom. Once a President exercises a power, he has established a precedent which will serve as a source of power to future Presidents.

The men who wrote the United States Constitution created a presidency which is not duplicated by any governmental system in the world. The American presidency is unique in the assemblage of powers vested in a single leader, unique in the way the leader is chosen, and equally unique in the relationship between the leader and the legislative branch of government.

The United States government is sometimes referred to as *presidential* in form, and is contrasted with the cabinet, or parliamentary, form of government. These labels refer primarily to the relationship between the executive and the legislature.

Distinctive features of the *presidential* form of government are that the chief executive is elected independently of the legislature, holds office for a fixed period, and is vested with extensive powers not subject to control by the legislature. The Chief Executive of the United States is, of course, of this classification, and the term, *presidential government* is descriptive of the government of the United States.

On the other hand, in a *cabinet* system of government, the chief executive and his cabinet are elected by the legislature from its own membership, hold office at the pleasure of the legislature, and may be voted out of office when they lose the support of a majority of the members of the legislature. In contrast with the American system of separation of powers of the executive and the legislature, supreme executive and political authority of the cabinet, or parliamentary, system of government rests with the legislature.

The greatest advantage of cabinet government over presidential government, according to many political scientists, is that when control of the legislature passes from one party to another, control of the executive branch passes with it.

Some observers have emphasized the weakness in American government which grows out of the fact that our political system makes it entirely possible for the nation to have a President of one political party and a Congress with either one or both houses controlled by the opposition party. This condition has actually existed throughout about half of the history of the United States and has often led to a course of indecisiveness in national policy.

I. ROLES OF THE UNITED STATES PRESIDENT

A. Chief Politician

1. Only public official politically responsible to the entire citizenship of the nation.
2. Influence over public opinion.
3. Party platform.
4. Party chief.
   a. Names national chairman of his party.
   b. Leader of his national party organization.
   c. Controller of patronage.
   d. However, he has little influence over selection of party nominees for congressional seats.
   e. Has limited influence with state and local party organizations.

B. Chief Administrator

1. Heads a civilian establishment of more than three million employees.
2. Has broad latitude in appointing, with Senate approval, his Cabinet, composed of heads of the major departments of government and others he may choose to designate as Cabinet members.
   a. Cabinet size is flexible.
   b. Cabinet may serve as advisory group only if President calls on it for advice.
   c. Major requisite for Cabinet members is that they be responsive to will of the President.
3. White House staff.
   a. Presidential assistants who serve in both advisory and high administrative roles.
   b. Number may vary with needs of a President.

C. Chief Legislator

1. Constitution requires President to address Congress on State of the Union, at which time he proposes needed legislation.
2. May call special sessions of Congress.
3. May send special messages to Congress.
4. Presidential veto may be used to nullify bills passed by Congress.
   a. Veto must come within ten days after President receives bill, if Congress is still in session.
   b. By two-thirds vote in both houses, Congress may pass bill into law over presidential veto.
   c. Veto must apply to whole bill, not just part of it.
5. Ordinance power is used by President to fill in details of laws passed by Congress.
   a. Rules issued by administrative agencies are an extension of President's ordinance powers.
   b. If Congress disapproves of such decisions, it may clarify its intent by subsequent legislation.

D. Foreign Policy Leader

1. Only official spokesman for nation in foreign-policy matters.
2. Directs all negotiations with foreign powers.
3. Controls diplomatic corps and armed forces.
4. Appoints all ambassadors.
5. Vested with complete power for recognition of foreign nations.
6. May negotiate treaties, which require Senate approval.
7. May make *executive agreements* with foreign powers.
   a. Such agreements have binding force of treaties.
   b. Senate approval not required.

8. Has full control over vast resources of State Department.
9. Need for swift action in secrecy caused authors of Constitution to vest such broad foreign-policy power in President.

E. Commander in Chief

1. Has complete power of command over armed forces in war and in peace.
2. Appoints and may dismiss any or all military officers.
3. Directs nation's defense planning.
4. Congress has important checks on military power of President.
   a. Raises armed forces, determining their number.
   b. Must appropriate money for war and defense expenditures.
   c. Enacts military regulations.
   d. Sets maximum size for the military.
   e. May exert controls through power of investigation.
   f. Only Congress may *declare* war, but President may commit military forces without such declaration, thus possibly making declaration of war inevitable.
5. During time of war, President's military powers are vastly expanded, as Congress yields to necessity for unified leadership.

F. Chief of State

1. Judicial authority gives President power to grant clemency for offenses against the United States.
2. Sole representative of United States at ceremonial functions.

II. POWERS OF THE PRESIDENT

A. In General

1. Major powers of the President are implied by the foregoing outline of presidential roles, but some elaboration is necessary.
2. Presidential powers are not isolated, as would be indicated by any discussion of the subject, but overlap and complement each other, making him a powerful leader without necessarily realizing at many times which particular power of office he is utilizing.
3. Many presidential powers grow out of custom and precedent and are not specifically delegated to him by the Constitution.

B. Executive Powers

1. Appointment.
   a. President may appoint, with advice and consent of the Senate, the principal officers of government.
   b. Applies to Cabinet members, top administrative officials, judges, diplomatic officials, members of regulatory agencies and others.
   c. Power specifically granted by Constitution, Article II, Section 2, Paragraph 2.
   d. While Senate is not in session, may make interim appointments to fill vacancies, but such appointments expire at the end of next Senate session unless confirmed.
   e. Appointment of "inferior officers" is provided for by statute, rather than by Constitution.
   f. Custom of senatorial courtesy has wrested much of the appointive power from the President.
   g. Presidential appointments of Cabinet members, ambassadors, and Supreme Court justices are seldom opposed by the Senate.

h. Constitution is vague concerning President's power of removal, but in practice, Cabinet members and top administrative officers serve at his pleasure.

2. Appointive power implies power to supervise activities of executive agencies through his appointees.

C. Legislative Power

1. Has grown especially fast during twentieth century.
2. Grows out of constitutional requirement that the President address Congress on State of the Union.
3. Power often overlooked because of more spectacular nature of President's executive actions.
4. As head of largest bureaucracy of specialists in the world, President is in key position to know, through subordinates, what legislation is needed.
5. President's power to gain legislative aims lies largely in State of Union recommendations and in bill originating with the administration and sponsored by friendly members of Congress.
6. When Congress balks at proposed legislation, and the President deems it important, he has a number of pressures he may apply to seek congressional cooperation.
   a. Special messages to Congress.
   b. Conferences with congressional leaders.
   c. Patronage manipulation.
   d. Appeals to the public over the heads of Congress.
7. A negative legislative power of the President is the executive veto, or the threat of veto.
   a. If he approves a measure passed by Congress, he may sign it, thus making it a law.
   b. If he disapproves of the measure in part, he may take no action, and it will become law without his signature in ten days.
   c. If he disapproves of entire bill passed by Congress, he may veto it, returning it to house of origin with reason for his disapproval.
   d. The "pocket veto rule" applies if Congress adjourns within ten days after sending the President a bill it has passed; by not signing it, the President applies a silent or "pocket" veto.
8. The President's ordinance power is an example of one type of legislative power he holds.
   a. Authority of the President and his administration to fill in the gaps of general legislation passed by Congress.
   b. If Congress disapproves of how this power is applied in a particular instance, it may clarify its intent by later legislation.
9. Extensive delegation of legislative powers is made to the President during time of war, because of the need for quick action and unified control.

D. Judicial Powers

1. Constitutional power to grant clemency.
   a. Pardon—does not deny the fact of a crime but relieves the convicted person of the necessity of paying the penalty.
   b. Parole—conditional pardon, whereby freedom is granted on assurance that certain conditions will be met.
   c. Commutation—reduction of penalty, such as substitution of life imprisonment for death penalty.
   d. Reprieve—stay of sentence, such as a grant of 60 days in which to prepare an appeal to a higher court.
   e. Amnesty—clemency granted to a group of people, such as forgiveness for rebellion against the United States.
2. Clemency power is vested in chief executive of most nations.
3. President grants more than 500 pardons each year.

E. Military Powers

1. Constitution, Article II, Section 2, designates the President as Commander in Chief of the army and navy and of the national guard when called into national service.
2. In peacetime, size of land force and number of air wings, for example, can only be recommended by President. Congress has last word.
3. In wartime, President's powers are vastly expanded; nation looks to him, rather than to Congress, for unified leadership.
4. Potentialities of war power were first explored by President Lincoln.
5. President shares war power with Congress, which must provide money, thus must approve of general conduct of war.

F. Diplomatic Powers

1. Ratifies treaties, with advice and consent of Senate.
2. May negotiate executive agreements without congressional approval.
3. Appoints ambassadors and other public ministers.
4. Recognizes foreign nations.
5. Has ultimate control of State Department activities.

G. Political Powers

1. National leader of his political party.
2. Responsible for naming national party chairman.
3. Molder of public opinion, with immediate access to public ear.

SELECTED TEST QUESTIONS

I. Multiple Choice

1. If Congress adjourns within ten days after final passage of a bill and the President takes no action on the bill, it:
   (a) becomes law without his signature; (b) dies, a victim of the pocket veto; (c) awaits presidential action till the next meeting of Congress; (d) is mailed to the congressmen at their homes for final action.
2. An effective tool of the President in bypassing the Senate role in treaty-making is:
   (a) the executive agreement; (b) senatorial courtesy; (c) the executive veto; (d) none of these.
3. Congress has wrested much patronage power from the President through the custom of:
   (a) overriding his vetoes; (b) senatorial courtesy; (c) cloture petitions; (d) impeachment.
4. In order to remove from office a member of his Cabinet, the President may:
   (a) seek permission of the Civil Service Commission; (b) seek permission of both houses of Congress; (c) seek permission of the Senate only; (d) act independently on his own conviction.
5. The number of presidential assistants with Cabinet rank is determined by:
   (a) the Constitution; (b) act of Congress; (c) the President, with permission of the Vice President and Speaker of the House; (d) the President.

II. True-False

1. Overriding a presidential veto requires a two-thirds majority vote in both houses of Congress.
2. Although the President's legislative power is great, it has shown little growth in the twentieth century.

3. Although only Congress may *declare* war, the President, as commander in chief may lead the nation into a position which makes a declaration of war almost inevitable.
4. Although the President may be a powerful leader, if one or both houses of Congress is controlled by the opposition political party, his power may be sharply reduced.
5. Throughout U.S. history, a general increase in the power of the President has been noted in spite of occasional temporary declines.

CHAPTER 18

The Presidential Establishment

INTRODUCTION

The President of the United States is the only elected official in the nation whose first concern must be the welfare of the entire nation. Well over one hundred million voters take part in his selection. Once innaugurated, the President has a power of command over a civilian bureaucracy which has long since numbered more than three million. Within limits, too, he has some power of command over an entire nation with a population exceeding two hundred million and a highly influential voice in determining the course of events throughout the entire Western world.

Much speculation surrounds the question of whether the United States presidency has become too much of a job to be handled by just one man. Because of the indescribable proportions of the job, a tremendous bureaucracy has built up under the President's nominal command within the national government. At times cumbersome and unresponsive, this bureaucracy is—at least in theory—subject to the command of the President.

No corner of the earth is without a representative of the United States government who makes periodic reports to Washington and who is subject to the influence of the President of the United States.

The President must make many decisions which have important impact on the course of world history. Custom and usage have been important in surrounding him with an elaborate assemblage of advisers. However, he is not obligated to honor their advice. Only he can make the crucial decisions, and he may take his advice where he finds it—even from his personal friends, his relatives, or his wife, if he so chooses. On his desk in the White House President Truman kept a small sign which read, "The Buck Stops Here." This sign is a dramatic, if terse, restatement of the fact that the President in many matters speaks with final authority for the entire nation, and he cannot share that responsibility with anyone. He may listen to as many advisers as he wishes, but the final decision must be his.

Most citizens are probably unaware that the expansive bureaucracy of the United States government includes the greatest assemblage of specialists ever known. From the Department of Agriculture to the Federal Bureau of Investigation, federal personnel include numerous public servants who are so highly specialized that only an organization so vast could find need for their full services.

I. THE PRESIDENT'S ADVISERS

A. The Cabinet

1. Heads of the major administrative departments.
2. Not provided for by Constitution.
3. Flexible in size.
4. At the end of 1972, eleven major departments were included in the Cabinet.
   a. State
   b. Treasury
   c. Defense
   d. Justice
   e. Interior

    f. Agriculture

    g. Commerce

    h. Labor

    i. Health, Education and Welfare

    j. Housing and Urban Development

    k. Transportation

5. Each member (Secretary) appointed by President with Senate confirmation.

6. Members serve at pleasure of President.

7. Has no collective authority or responsibility.

8. Role in national government depends on President's preferences.

    a. Frequency of meetings determined entirely by President.

    b. Advisory capacity sometimes emphasized.

    c. Often viewed merely as heads of administrative departments.

9. Clientele interests tend to exert pressures on policy direction of each major department.

B. Personal Staff

1. Attract more public notice than other presidential advisers.

2. Responsible for handling routine of office.

3. Number of assistants has increased dramatically in recent decades.

4. Senior assistants work with matters of more than routine nature.

    a. Press relations.

    b. Speech writing.

    c. Economic planning.

    d. Patronage.

    e. National security.

    f. Congressional relations.

    g. Office appointments.

    h. Executive staff recruitment.

5. Less subject to political influence than Cabinet members.

6. Different Presidents organize assistants in different organizational patterns, use them differently.

C. Executive Office of the President

1. *National Security Council.*

    a. Created by National Security Act of 1947.

    b. Formal advisory body in foreign policy, military policy.

    c. Consists of President, Secretaries of State and Defense, Director of Emergency Planning.

    d. Created in response to needs of Cold War.

2. *Office of Management and Budget (OMB)*

    a. Formerly known as Bureau of the Budget.

    b. Major purpose is to help President direct and control executive branch.

    c. Director appointed by President without Senate confirmation.

    d. Office dates back to 1921 and congressional passage of Budget and Accounting Act.

    e. Office has three major functions.

        (1) Formulation and execution of federal budget.

        (2) Assistance in improving organization and management of executive branch.

        (3) Assistance in executive handling of legislative matters.

3. *Domestic Council.*

    a. Created in 1970 by President Nixon.

   b. Cabinet-level forum.
   c. Membership includes President, Vice President, heads of most Cabinet departments, agency heads selected by President.
   d. Advises President on domestic matters.
4. *Council of Economic Advisers.*
   a. Created by Employment Act of 1946.
   b. Helps President prepare economics report for each regular session of Congress.
   c. Composed of three members appointed by President with advice and consent of Senate.
   d. Primary interest is recommending policies directed toward achieving maximum employment, production, and purchasing power.
5. *Office of Science and Technology.*
   a. Headed, since 1962, by the special assistant to the President for science and technology.
   b. Helps President evaluate proposals from operating agencies.

D. Advisers from Outside the Federal Government

1. Personal friends.
   a. Affords President flexible source of counsel.
   b. Utilized by most Presidents.
   c. May have originated with Andrew Jackson's "kitchen cabinet."
   d. Insures relationship of personal trust and understanding.
   e. May serve as sounding boards for tentative proposals.
2. Task forces and commissions.
   a. Opportunity to utilize nongovernmental figures for group advice in policy formulation.
   b. First used by President Theodore Roosevelt.
   c. Major advantage is ability to approach problems without institutional prejudices.
   d. Commonly serve on *ad hoc* basis (to study and report on a single problem).
   e. Major disadvantage is that such groups are powerless to see to it that recommendations are pursued.

II. OVERSEEING THE BUREAUCRACY

A. Executive Control Factors

1. Minimizing patronage promises.
2. Cross-specialization assignments.
3. Selection of major department heads for personal responsiveness.
4. Selection of agency heads on basis of personal commitment.
5. President can never be assured of control of independent regulatory commissions.
6. Major problem of President often is gaining compliance with his will by agency staffs.

B. Executive Organization and Reorganization

1. Organization of executive branch is constantly changing.
2. When Congress creates new government function, directorship must be worked into executive establishment.
3. Constant pressures urge creation of new Cabinet departments.
4. Clientele groups exert constant pressure to gain advantageous structure in administrative departments.
5. Continuing reexamination of executive structure has two primary goals.
   a. To reduce governmental costs.
   b. To minimize President's responsibility for overall management.

6. Students identify three principal weaknesses in executive control.
   a. President expected to supervise personally too many varied operations.
   b. Congress has made many agencies partially independent of the President.
   c. Congress has often undercut presidential authority by detailing how executive officials must perform.
7. Congressmen, jealous of own prerogatives, are often uninterested in executive reorganization which will strengthen President's control.
8. Reorganization Act of 1949 has increased executive control of administrative structure.
   a. Grew out of recommendations of first Hoover Commission.
   b. Provides that presidential plan for reorganization will take effect unless Congress rejects it within 60 days.
   c. Since 1949, more than 80 reorganization plans have been submitted to Congress, three-fourths accepted.

C. Top Executives

1. About 500 political executives appointed by President.
2. About 5,000 career executives as professional administrators remaining in service despite political changes.
3. Political executive positions characterized by brief tenure, which undercuts effective political leadership in federal agencies.
4. Importance of top political executives is role in keeping bureaucracy responsive to will of the President.
5. Four major obstacles hinder the recruitment of top executive talent.
   a. Salaries do not match those offered by private business.
   b. Nongovernmental experience is often inadequate preparation for executive work in government.
   c. Often-intangible goals of government programs not comparable to goals observed in business.
   d. Conflict-of-interest laws.

D. Career Executives

1. Service and tenure are tied to no political commitments.
2. Expected to retain positions when administrations change.
3. Expected to have political skill without partisan involvement.
4. After many years in office, career executives tend to become unresponsive to political executives over them.

SELECTED TEST QUESTIONS

I. Multiple Choice

1. The number of major departments included in the Cabinet at the end of 1972 was:
   (a) twenty; (b) forty-two; (c) fourteen; (d) eleven.
2. Dismissal of a Cabinet member from office depends on:
   (a) constitutional provision; (b) statutory provision; (c) approval by the Senate; (d) independent decision by the President.
3. A key member of the executive establishment who may be appointed by the President without Senate approval is the:
   (a) Secretary of State; (b) Director of the Office of Management and Budget; (c) Secretary of Defense; (d) Secretary of the Treasury.

4. When the Cabinet votes on a major policy issue placed before it, the President is:
(a) still free to make independent decision; (b) obligated to follow advice of Cabinet majority; (c) obligated to follow advice only if Cabinet is unanimous; (d) obligated to place Cabinet decision before Congress for action.

5. Career executives in the federal bureaucracy are expected to:
(a) lend political support to the President during election campaigns; (b) resign with a change of administration; (c) avoid partisan involvement and remain in office when administrations change; (d) provide the "loyal opposition" to the administration in office.

II. True-False

1. Veteran career executives have a tendency to become highly expert in their work and to become unresponsive to political superiors.
2. The Reorganization Act of 1949 eased presidential problems with executive reorganization.
3. The Budget and Accounting Act of 1921 weakened the role of the President in influencing formulation of the national budget.
4. The National Security Council determines national policy in the area of military planning.
5. The Constitution did not specify how many Cabinet departments were to be created.

CHAPTER 19

Courts, Justice, and the Law

INTRODUCTION

Under the Articles of Confederation, the national government had no court system. In a sense, therefore, it was dependent for its very existence and effectiveness on decisions reached in 13 separate systems of state courts. Aware of this weakness in the central government, the Founding Fathers sought to remedy it by the provisions they wrote into Article III of the Constitution.

The Constitution actually makes specific provision for only one court—the Supreme Court of the United States. It authorizes Congress to create such other courts as Congress might consider necessary. Fulfilling this mandate, the first Congress enacted the Judiciary Act of 1789, which created two levels of inferior *constitutional* courts—the United States District Courts, or so-called *trial* courts, and the United States Circuit Courts of Appeals, so called because the judges traveled from place to place to hear appeals from the trial courts.

From time to time Congress has found it necessary to create other courts—courts of a specialized nature, which are referred to as *legislative* courts.

An important characteristic of all federal courts is that the judges are appointed. Judges of the constitutional courts—Supreme Court, Courts of Appeals, and District Courts—are appointed to serve a lifetime tenure. Judges of legislative courts are appointed to serve terms fixed by Congress.

A significant feature of the United States judicial system is the tremendous power which it may exercise. It is the most powerful court system in the world. Some writers have noted that the powers of the federal courts have long since surpassed the powers of Congress, and evidence can be produced to support this view.

Overseas observers have often found it difficult to understand the awesome power of the United States Supreme Court. The root of that power lies in the fact that the Supreme Court is the final authority in interpreting the Constitution, and the Constitution is the supreme law of the land. Since 1803, the Supreme Court has exercised the power of *judicial review*, the power to declare an act of Congress void because it conflicts with the Court's interpretation of the Constitution.

Does this extreme power vested in the judiciary pose a threat to democratic values and institutions? Some critics declare emphatically that it does. Such power in the hands of men separated from the electoral process and protected by lifetime tenure is sometimes said to be a negation of the basic concept of democracy. If the electoral process is taken as the basic feature of democracy, then this is undoubtedly true. But if the concept of due process of law is seen as the basic democratic feature, then few would fault the federal courts for their respectful adherence to this concept of the essence of justice.

Most judges in the state courts are elected to office, thus making them at least nominally subject to the whims of public opinion. Associate Justice Brennan of the U.S. Supreme Court is perhaps the most prominent of the many critics who have pointed to the frequent disregard of due process considerations evident in decisions reached by some state courts.

Some conventional Americans take pride in declaring that, "Ours is a system of laws, not of men." Probably no greater shred of nonsense has ever been uttered. Laws are made by men, enforced by men, interpreted by men. Our system, like all political systems, is a system of laws *and* men. Judges *do* make law. They could not function without making law.

107

The American legal system is based on the concept of *case law*. This means that the courts are guided by *precedent* in determining the rights of parties to a legal dispute. This is also called the principle of *stare decisis* (let the decision stand) and the courts naturally try to avoid reversing principles established by past decisions.

It has been pointed out many times, however, that enough precedents exist to enable a court in a given instance to support either of two conflicting arguments with adequate precedent.

I. TYPES OF LEGAL SYSTEMS

A. Code Law

1. Common to many nations of Europe and Latin America.
2. Characterized by legal *codes* which attempt to state as clearly as possible what the law is.
3. Person has merely to read the law to know what his rights are.
4. Exemplified in the United States at the local level of government, with its traffic codes, building codes, etc.
5. Each case is judged on its own merits.

B. Case Law

1. One must look to precedent to find the law—what have the courts said in the past?
2. Common to English-speaking peoples.
3. Looking to past, it is generally thought of as conservative legal system.

II. TYPES OF LAW

A. Constitutional Law

1. Takes precedent over other types.
2. May be written or unwritten.
3. Final interpretation rests with U.S. Supreme Court.

B. Statutory Law

1. Law made by legislative bodies, representing the people.
2. Inferior to constitutional law.
3. May include treaties and executive orders.
4. Public policy stated in general terms.

C. Common Law

1. Inherited by American legal system from English judicial practice.
2. Finds its expression at state level in 49 states (Louisiana excepted).
3. Commonly defined as judge-made law.
4. There is no federal common law.

D. Equity

1. System of judge-made law.
2. Originated in England.
3. Seeks to provide *preventive* measures before remedy is needed.
4. Injunction to prohibit act which threatens irreparable harm is commonest example of equity writ.

E. Admiralty

1. Applied only by federal judges in the United States.
2. Adjudicates disputes rising out of commerce on the high seas and navigable waters of the United States.
3. Involves considerations of international law.

F. Administrative Law

1. Rises out of rules and decisions of administrators.
2. Especially important in involvement of independent regulatory commissions.
3. Administrative rules and decisions may be reviewed by federal judges.
4. Question of administrative authority often arises.

III. OTHER TYPES OF LAW

A. Criminal Law

1. Mostly statutory.
2. Prescribes punishment for offenses against the public order.
3. Government primarily responsible for enforcement.
4. Mostly of concern to state governments, acting within their police powers.

B. Civil Law

1. Establishes legal relationships between individuals.
2. Defines individual legal rights.
3. Seeks to provide remedies for transgressions growing out of relationships between individuals.

C. Adversary System

1. Characteristic of legal system in United States.
2. Courtroom is viewed as arena of combat, in which contending parties do best to convince court of righteousness of their respective claims.
3. Based on theory that truth grows out of unfettered clash of contending views.

IV. PROPER ROLE OF JUDGES — TWO VIEWS

A. Activism

1. Holds that judge should use his position to promote desirable social ends.
2. Concerned with "reasonableness" of legislative and executive acts.

B. Self-Restraint

1. Holds that judges should defer to legislative and executive branches.
2. Concerned with legitimacy of procedures, rather than reasonableness of substance.
3. Often referred to as "strict constructionism."

V. FEDERAL JUDICIAL STRUCTURE

A. Constitutional Courts

1. United States Supreme Court.
   a. Only court specifically created by the Constitution.
   b. Number of justices not fixed by Constitution.

    c. Today has a Chief Justice and eight associate justices.

    d. Number of justices has varied throughout history.

    e. Has *original* and *appellate* jurisdiction.

      (1) Original jurisdiction.

        (a) Controversies heard by Supreme Court without first being heard by inferior court.

        (b) Applies to "all cases affecting ambassadors, other public ministers and consuls, and those in which a state shall be a party."

        (c) Congress may not alter original jurisdiction.

      (2) Appellate jurisdiction.

        (a) Applies to review of cases tried and decided by other federal courts and administrative agencies.

        (b) Applies to review of decisions of highest state courts in which federal question is involved.

        (c) Congress may alter appellate jurisdiction.

  2. United States Courts of Appeals.

    a. Eleven courts encompassing geographical regions of the United States.

    b. Hear appeals from United States District Courts.

    c. Review and enforce actions of some administrative agencies.

  3. United States District Courts.

    a. Trial courts of national judicial system.

    b. Jurisdiction divided among 88 judicial districts in United States.

    c. Each state has from one to four federal judicial districts.

    d. Each judicial district is assigned 1-24 district judges.

  4. Special Constitutional Courts.

    a. Differ from Supreme Court, Courts of Appeals, and District Courts in basic sense that they do not have general jurisdiction.

    b. Similar to other constitutional courts in that judges have lifetime tenure.

    c. Jurisdiction is restricted to specialized area.

    d. Examples are U.S. Court of Claims, Customs Court, Court of Customs and Patent Appeals.

B. Legislative Courts

  1. Congress many create other courts of limited jurisdiction which lie outside the structure of *constitutional* courts.

  2. Major difference from constitutional courts is that judges serve for fixed terms, rather than lifetime tenure.

  3. Example is United States Court of Military Appeals.

C. Administrative Tribunals

  1. Exercise quasi-judicial power in carrying out functions of "independent" regulatory agencies.

  2. Terms and tenure of administrative adjudicators are set by Congress.

  3. Rulings may be reviewed by constitutional courts of general jurisdiction.

  4. Examples of such quasi-judicial agencies include the Interstate Commerce Commission, Federal Trade Commission, Securities and Exchange Commission.

VI. SELECTION OF FEDERAL JUDGES

A. Political Influences

  1. Judicial appointments are based on patronage considerations.

  2. Predominantly, Presidents select judges of own political party.

3. Men selected for judgeships have commonly been active servants of party interests.

4. President has relatively free hand in selection of Supreme Court justices.

5. The custom of senatorial courtesy gives a senator veto over appointment of judge to serve in his state—if the senator and the President are of the same party.

6. In any event, the senators of the state in which an appointment is to be made must be consulted.

B. Other Influences

1. Candidates for judgeships may apply political pressures for their appointments.

2. The American Bar Association has long sought a voice in the appointment and confirmation of judges, scoring varying degrees of success with different Presidents.

3. State and federal judges often exert pressures of their own.

4. Political party leaders are eager to influence this choice area of patronage.

VII. THE U.S. SUPREME COURT IN OPERATION

A. When the Court Sits

1. Regular sessions are held from October through June.

2. Court hears oral arguments in alternate two-week periods.

3. After hearing arguments for two weeks, the Court adjourns for two weeks to consider cases and prepare opinions.

4. At least six justices must participate in each decision.

5. Cases are decided by a majority vote.

6. Three kinds of opinions are issued.

    a. Majority opinions—legally binding opinions of the Court.

    b. Concurring opinions—agreeing with the majority's conclusion, but disagreeing with how it is reached or stated.

    c. Dissenting opinions—disagreeing with the majority's conclusion and stating arguments in rebuttal to majority opinion.

B. Cases Which Reach the Court

1. Cases may reach the Court by any of three routes.

    a. Original jurisdiction.

        (1) Relatively rare.

        (2) Cases involving representatives of foreign nations and those in which a state is a party.

    b. Appeal.

        (1) Cases in which a lower court has invalidated a state or federal law.

        (2) Such cases go to the Supreme Court as a matter of right, unless the Court dismisses them for lack of significance.

        (3) *Certiorari.*

            (a) Writ of *certiorari* is an order by a court of appellate jurisdiction to a court of inferior jurisdiction, directing that the record of a case be sent up for review.

            (b) Four justices must concur before the Supreme Court will issue a write of *certiorari.*

            (c) The Supreme Court justices have full discretion in deciding which cases they will consider on *certiorari.*

            (d) Most of the highly significant cases reaching the Supreme Court come on *certiorari.*

VIII. THE JUDGES AS PROTECTORS OF THE CONSTITUTION

A. Judicial Role

1. Judges are guided by the Constitution, basic law of the land, in determining the legitimacy of any challenged law or administrative action.
2. Laws and treaties are of secondary, but still great, importance in guiding judicial determinations.
3. Judges will avoid ruling on issue of constitutionality if another method of settling a controversy is open.
4. Federal courts will accept only those cases in which a legitimate controversy is present.

B. Judicial Review

1. Power of a court to nullify a legislative act which it holds to be in conflict with the Constitution.
2. Only in the United States do courts exercise the power of judicial review.
3. Not specifically vested in federal courts by the Constitution.
4. Concept of judicial review was created by Chief Justice John Marshal with his opinion in the case of *Marbury v. Madison* (1803).
5. Adds greatly to powers exercised by courts in the United States.
6. Lends flexibility to a government operating under a written constitution.
7. Highest court in each of 50 states exercises similar power over acts of state legislatures.

SELECTED TEST QUESTIONS

I. Multiple Choice

1. The precedent of judicial review was established by the U.S. Supreme Court in the case of:
   (a) *Marbury v. Madison;* (b) *McCulloch v. Maryland;* (c) *Barron v. Baltimore;* (d) *Fletcher v. Peck.*
2. The minimum number of justices who must participate in a case before the Supreme Court is:
   (a) nine; (b) six; (c) seven; (d) five.
3. It is generally agreed that the greatest number of important questions reach the Supreme Court on:
   (a) original jurisdiction; (b) writ of appeal; (c) writ of *certiorari;* (d) none of these.
4. Judicial activism refers to:
   (a) a judge's impatience with trial lawyers; (b) judicial preoccupation with the letter of the Constitution; (c) judicial deference to legislative discretion; (d) use of judicial power to pursue desirable social aims.
5. Judicial self-restraint refers to:
   (a) judicial deference to the *political* branches of government; (b) an inclination by the Supreme Court to rule for the national government in conflicts with states; (c) efforts by judges to keep their opinions from running too long.

II. True-False

1. The United States Constitution provided for only one federal court specifically.
2. The Constitution provides that nine judges shall sit on the Supreme Court.
3. Partisan politics is an important consideration in the appointment of federal judges.
4. *Stare decisis* refers to judicial practice under a system of code law.
5. Only in the United States do courts exercise the power of judicial review.

CHAPTER 20

United States Foreign Policy

INTRODUCTION

Prior to World War II, when the United States was a relatively minor power in the world, its foreign policy was a secondary consideration in the overall picture of national government activity. Although growing, U.S. interests abroad were limited, the army was small, and military spending was moderate.

However, with the development of nuclear arms and the rapid expansion of American interests abroad, the nation emerged from the war in the undisputed role of most powerful country on earth. Much of the world looked to the United States for leadership in grappling with a broad variety of problems. Ever since, foreign policy has loomed large as a factor in the nation's security and prosperity. Foreign markets for American manufacturers are commonly considered important to the maintenance of a high level of employment in the United States.

The men who wrote the United States Constitution had had little experience with the conduct of foreign affairs. But they were convinced that the executive must have a strong hand in the formulation of foreign policy. So they made the American President the architect of his nation's foreign policy. The President must have much help, of course, and he can do little without the cooperation of Congress, but the final responsibility remains his. He cannot delegate the final decision-making function.

To help him carry out this responsibility, the President has the assistance of a vast corps of diplomatic agents living in every part of the world and maintaining constant communication with the White House through the Department of State. The Secretary of State, appointed by the President, is responsible for seeing to it that these channels of communication are maintained and that matters which require top-level policy decisions are brought to the attention of the President. At the same time, he must be the alter ego of the President by being able to shield the President from personal involvement in foreign-policy matters of lesser importance. This means that he must be able to handle the routine of the office in such a way as to keep American foreign policy moving toward goals and in channels prescribed by the President.

I. CHANGING FACE OF THE MODERN WORLD

A. Technical Progress

1. Nuclear energy.
2. Supersonic air travel.
3. Space exploration.
4. Satellite communications.
5. Many other radical technological changes.

B. Emphasis on Human Welfare

1. Concern for agricultural advancement among primitive peoples.
2. Concern for industrial development in underdeveloped nations.
3. Concern for improved medical-hospital facilities in more remote areas of world.

C. Political Change

1. Economic and political integration of Europe with strong encouragement from United States.
2. Decline of colonialism throughout the world.
3. Reascension of Japan.
4. Emergence of China as great world power.

II. WHO MAKES FOREIGN POLICY?

A. Basic Tools Available

1. Information.
2. Negotiation.
3. Persuasion.
4. Propaganda.
5. Economic assistance.
6. Military assistance.
7. Threats of armed force.
8. Use of armed force.

B. Men Who Use the Tools

1. The President.
   a. Has final responsibility for formation and direction.
   b. Has sole power to recognize foreign nations.
   c. Appoints Secretary of State and top officials in State Department.
   d. Appoints Secretary of Defense and top officials in Defense Department.
   e. As Commander in Chief, has access to vast military power of United States.
   f. As Chief Executive, has broad powers over U.S. imports and exports.
   g. Has advantage of being able to act swiftly, secretly, and decisively.
2. *Secretary of State.*
   a. Appointed by President.
   b. Responsible directly to President.
   c. Discretionary authority only that granted by President.
   d. Usually most prominent member of Cabinet.
   e. Oversees day-to-day operation of Department of State.
   f. Effectiveness depends largely on public opinion and power relationship between President and Congress.
3. *Secretary of Defense.*
   a. Importance of foreign policy hinges on priority of national security in foreign-policy considerations.
   b. Provides channel of communication between President and defense establishment.
4. Departmental and agency specialists.
   a. At least 50 agencies are concerned directly with U.S. foreign policy.
   b. President has full freedom in selecting specialists from the bureaucracy to advise him on foreign policy.
   c. Such areas as finance and agriculture are prime examples.
   d. Loyalties of such advisers are divided between foreign-policy goals and goals of respective departments.
5. *Special Assistant for National Security Affairs.*
   a. Many Presidents have used special assistants as foreign-policy advisers.

  b. Only recently has the office been formalized with a large staff of experts.

  c. Keeps President informed of important developments of pertinence to American foreign policy.

  d. Office sometimes viewed as conflicting with role of State Department.

 6. Intelligence personnel.

  a. State Department Bureau of Intelligence and Research.

  b. Defense Intelligence Agency.

  c. National Security Agency.

  d. Atomic Energy Commission.

  e. Federal Bureau of Investigation.

  f. *Central Intelligence Agency.*

   (1) Probably most important of the six.

   (2) Employs more than 15,000 persons.

   (3) Operates on classified budget which exceeds $600 million a year.

   (4) Has played aggressive role in such ventures as deposing unfriendly foreign governments.

 7. *National Security Council.*

  a. Created in 1947.

  b. Intended to aid the President in coordinating and integrating all national security efforts.

  c. Intelligence arm is the Central Intelligence Agency.

  d. Membership includes the President, Secretary of State, Secretary of Defense, Director of the Office of Emergency Planning, and others the President may appoint.

  e. Has been used in various fashions by different Presidents.

III. PUBLIC OPINION AND FOREIGN POLICY

A. The Three Publics

 1. Mass public.

  a. Constitutes 75-85 percent of adult population.

  b. Generally uninformed of foreign affairs.

 2. Attentive public.

  a. About 10 percent of adult population.

  b. Actively interested in foreign policy.

 3. Opinion leaders.

  a. Perhaps 5 percent of the adult population.

  b. Active in influencing foreign-policy opinions of others.

B. Does Public Opinion Influence Foreign Policy?

 1. Walter Lippmann, contemporary American writer, has proposed that public opinion has caused American leaders to make crucial mistakes in foreign policy, when the leaders themselves knew better than what public opinion demanded.

 2. Alexis de Tocqueville, French intellectual, pointed out as early as 1835 that public-opinion influence on foreign policy was one of the basic weaknesses of the theory of democracy.

 3. Recognizing the importance of public opinion, the Department of State makes an effort to measure and mold public opinion.

 4. The President tries to win public support for his own foreign-policy objectives by making frequent addresses on the subject.

C. Interest-Group Influence on Foreign Policy

1. Studies have shown that interest groups seem to have little influence on foreign policy.
2. Policy-makers' anticipation of interest-group reactions may have great bearing on decisions, but is impossible to measure.

D. Political Parties and Foreign Policy

1. Parties are hesitant to take foreign-policy positions.
2. When parties do take stands, they are usually obscured by vagueness.
3. Most Americans prefer that foreign policy remain nonpolitical.
4. The concept of *bipartisanship* in foreign policy has had much support since World War II.

E. Congressional Influence on Foreign Policy

1. Foreign-policy influence of Congress is essentially negative.
   a. Congress cannot formulate foreign policy as such.
   b. Congress can undermine the President's foreign policy.
   c. Congress can refuse to appropriate money needed to pursue President's foreign-policy objectives.
2. The President does frequently confer with congressional leaders, especially the chairman of the Senate Committee on Foreign Relations, on foreign-policy matters.

SELECTED TEST QUESTIONS

I. Multiple Choice

1. In formulating foreign policy, the President must consult the:
   (a) Secretary of State; (b) Secretary of Defense; (c) both; (d) neither.
2. The Central Intelligence agency is an arm of the:
   (a) Department of State; (b) Department of Defense; (c) Office of Emergency Planning; (d) National Security Council.
3. Foreign-policy advice with the least bureaucratic prejudice might be expected to be given the President by:
   (a) the Secretary of State; (b) Secretary of Defense; (c) departmental specialists; (d) the Special Assistant to the President for National Security Affairs.
4. Disinterest and a lack of information about foreign policy is characteristic of:
   (a) a small minority of Americans; (b) about one-fourth of the American people; (c) about half the American adults; (d) about 75-85 percent of American adults.
5. Foreign policy assumed a role of unprecedented importance for the United States:
   (a) during the Civil War; (b) at the end of World War I; (c) during the Great Depression; (d) at the end of World War II.

II. True-False

1. The authors of the United States Constitution intended that the President should have a strong hand in the area of foreign policy.
2. The President and the Secretary of State share the ultimate responsibility for foreign policy about equally.
3. The President usually ignores public attitudes toward foreign policy.
4. The role of Congress in formulating foreign policy is essentially negative in the sense that it may not formulate policy, but may often block the President's proposals.
5. Studies have shown that interest groups have little direct effect on foreign policy.

CHAPTER 21

Conducting Foreign Relations

INTRODUCTION

Development of nuclear arms in the past quarter century has added new emphasis to the need for major world powers to keep well informed on the aims and activities of other nations and to keep other nations informed on their own aims and activities. The thought of a nuclear holocaust sparked by misunderstanding poses an awesome specter.

The President may make foreign policy through his speeches, press conferences, military command, and behind-the-scenes maneuvering. Congress may implement the President's foreign policy pronouncements by providing the money, men, and material required.

But what about the enormous job of maintaining reliable two-way communications links with nations in the far corners of the world? Who performs the task of making sure that the President understands the intentions of other world powers and that their leaders understand the intentions of the United States? Certainly the President himself has no time to spend on the details of day-to-day intercourse with other nations. Primary responsibility for execution of the nation's foreign policy and keeping the channels of communication open to all parts of the world rests with the United States Department of State.

I. BASIC FUNCTIONS AND ORGANIZATION OF THE STATE DEPARTMENT

A. Routine Functions

1. To keep the President informed of important developments throughout the world which might have policy implications.
2. To advise the President and assist him in forming and executing foreign policy.
3. Through U.S. embassies abroad and overseas embassies in Washington, to maintain reliable communications.
4. To conduct diplomatic and trade negotiations with foreign states and to oversee private trade negotiations with foreign nations.
5. To coordinate all official activities by men and agencies in the U.S. government which have foreign-policy implications.

B. Formal Organization

1. General characteristics.
   a. In state of constant growth and reorganization.
   b. Often criticized for its size.
   c. Actually is smallest of the Cabinet departments.
2. Directorship.
   a. Secretary of State performs policy-making and advisory functions.
   b. Secretary is assisted by two under secretaries and two deputy secretaries.
   c. Fifteen assistant secretaries.
   d. Several hundred specialists.
   e. *Policy-Planning Council.*

117

3. Executive secretariat.
   a. Coordinates policy-making and advisory functions.
   b. Maintains Operations Center.
4. Dual operational organization.
   a. Ten functional bureaus headed by assistant secretaries.
     (1) Congressional Affairs.
     (2) Economic Affairs.
     (3) Educational and Cultural Affairs
     (4) Intelligence Research
     (5) International Scientific and Technological Affairs.
     (6) Legal Adviser.
     (7) Organizations Affairs.
     (8) Politico-Military Affairs.
     (9) Public Affairs.
    (10) Security and Consular Affairs.
   b. Five geographic bureaus headed by assistant secretaries.
     (1) African.
     (2) East Asian.
     (3) European.
     (4) Inter-American.
     (5) South Asian.

C. Specialized Agencies

1. *Agency for International Development (AID)*
   a. Loosely tied to State Department.
   b. Directs U.S. economic and technical assistance to other nations.
   c. Participates in military aid programs.
   d. Has been reorganized and renamed many times.
2. *United States Information Agency (USIA)*
   a. Director appointed by President.
   b. Offices separate from State Department.
   c. Creates *Voice of America* broadcasts in 40 languages.
   d. Publishes magazines in 27 languages.
   e. Produces and distributes books overseas.
   f. Maintains overseas libraries.
3. *Arms Control and Disarmament Agency (ACDA)*
   a. Created in 1961 to study long-range disarmament problems.
   b. Director reports to Secretary of State and President.
   c. Main functions are research and briefing of U.S. disarmament negotiators.

II. UNITED STATES REPRESENTATIVES ABROAD

A. Size and Scope of Program

1. Ambassadorial service older than Constitution.
2. The United States now has 300 active missions abroad.
3. Diplomatic posts in most of world's capital cities.
4. U.S. missions with international organizations.
5. Heads of foreign missions appointed by President with Senate approval.

6. Three ranks of foreign mission heads.
   a. Ambassador.
   b. Minister.
   c. Chargé d'affaires.

B. Diplomatic Agents

1. Formerly ambassadors were sent only to major nations, lesser officers to smaller countries.
2. The United States sends ambassadors to almost all recognized nations today.
3. Career foreign-service officers have replaced political appointees at head of most U.S. embassies.
4. Chiefly interested in political and economic relations.
5. Consuls, however, are mainly concerned with individuals.

C. Quality of Diplomatic Agents

1. In early American history, high-caliber men were appointed to diplomatic posts.
2. Early in nineteenth century, diplomatic posts came to be considered political rewards.
3. Wealthy men were commonly preferred as ambassadors because of low salaries and high cost of maintaining embassy.
4. Consular offices were highly lucrative.
5. In 1924, the **Rogers Act** reformed and reorganized diplomatic service, providing for career foreign-service officers.
6. Foreign service was further strengthened by the **Foreign Service Act of 1946.**

D. The Modern United States Foreign Service

1. Field representatives of U.S. government overseas.
2. Serves State Department and other governmental agencies.
3. Carries out U.S. policy under direction of Secretary of State.
4. Major function is gathering data.
5. Protects Americans and American interests.
6. Service has own training school.

III. U.S. PARTICIPATION IN INTERNATIONAL ORGANIZATIONS

A. Scope and Purpose of Participation

1. Membership in more than 200 international organizations is major phase of American diplomatic relations.
2. International activism of the United States today in sharp contrast with isolationism before World War II.

B. Organization of American States (OAS)

1. Alliance of 24 American nations.
2. Established in 1948 with the **Charter of Punte del Este.**
3. Responsible for fostering economic and social progress in Western hemisphere.

C. United Nations

1. Basic purposes to maintain world peace and promote social and economic progress.
2. Like most members, the United States keeps permanent diplomatic mission at U.N. headquarters in New York.

3. Chief of U.S. mission to the U.N. has Cabinet status.
4. The United States is one of five members of U.N. Security Council, which has major peace-keeping responsibilities.

SELECTED TEST QUESTIONS

I. Multiple Choice

1. Among the Cabinet departments, the State Department is the:
   (a) largest; (b) smallest; (c) second largest; (d) fifth largest.
2. The Director of the United States Information Agency is appointed by:
   (a) the Secretary of State; (b) Congress; (c) the President; (d) the Civil Service System.
3. The number of diplomatic posts maintained abroad by the United States is:
   (a) 25; (b) 50; (c) 150; (d) 300.
4. The United Nations organ with major peace-keeping responsibilities is the:
   (a) Security Council; (b) General Assembly; (c) International Court of Justice; (d) Economic and Social Council.
5. The number of nations participating in the Organization of American States is:
   (a) 18; (b) 56; (c) 131; (d) 24.

II. True-False

1. The United States is a member of more than 200 international organizations.
2. The nineteenth century is noted for the high quality of U.S. representatives to foreign governments.
3. The majority of chiefs of U.S. missions abroad are career foreign-service officers.
4. U.S. consular officers overseas are primarily concerned with trade relations.
5. In 1924, the Rogers Act reorganized and reformed the diplomatic service.

CHAPTER 22

National Defense

INTRODUCTION

The United States is the only nation on earth which has ever unleashed nuclear power as a destructive instrument of war. After the holocaust of Hiroshima, where American nuclear war power was first tested, a mere seven years were to pass before both the United States and Russia were to both have atomic bombs and the ability to deliver them as a destructive agent against the other.

Thus was painted the picture of national security for both nations for all the years that have since passed. Although the two nations were allies in World War I and again in World War II, the ideological discord between dictatorship and representative democracy, between socialism and capitalism, was seemingly heightened by the development of a new and awesome weapon. Distrust has been the dominant characteristic of U.S.-Soviet relations ever since. So much so that one hears common talk of a *bipolarized* world. The term *preventive war* was popularized for a time in the United States.

Obviously frightened by the demonstrated aggressions and suspected motivations of the other, both the United States and Russia diverted massive amounts of their productive potential to making preparations for a war each feared the other might start.

Literally millions of Americans today are employed, either directly or indirectly, in jobs which exist only because of this great mutual fear between East and West. As might be expected, a small enterprising group of Americans amassed wealth selling underground bomb shelters to frightened home owners.

For a few anxious days in October, 1962, it seemed as if the worst fears were on the brink of fulfillment. United States aerial reconnaissance revealed that Russia was in the process of establishing a missile base in Cuba, which could have served as a launching pad for nuclear bombs aimed with deadly accuracy. The nation's heart skipped a beat as President Kennedy readied the U.S. nuclear offensive and warned Russian Premier Khruschev that any attack on the United States would be answered by an attack, not on Cuba, but on the Soviet heartland. A naval blockade was thrown up around Cuba which diverted Russian ships carrying additional weapons to that base. As one popular writer put it, this marked an "eyeball-to-eyeball" confrontation between the chiefs of the two greatest powers on earth. The Russian leader blinked, and the world could breathe more easily.

I. CIVILIAN MILITARY CONTROL

A. Executive

1. As Commander in Chief, President commissions all officers.
2. Secretary of Defense is President's civilian Cabinet-rank lieutenant presiding over military establishment.

B. Legislative

1. Congress sets limits on size of military.
2. Congress controls the "purse strings" of military spending.
3. Congress may investigate irregular activities in the military.
4. Only Congress may formally declare war, but President may send troops to any part of world without congressional approval.

C. Department of Defense

1. Housed in the Pentagon, world's largest office building.
2. Headquarters of Secretary of Defense and top command for all U.S. armed forces.
3. Clearinghouse for budget of $75 billion a year.

D. Inter-Service Relationships

1. Until 1947, land and naval forces were administered separately through Department of War and Department of Navy, with little coordination.
2. Lack of coordination during World War II led to clamor for unification of services.
3. *Unification Act of 1947* created three separate sub-departments, army, navy, and air force under control of Secretary of Defense, a newly created Cabinet position, compromised many differences between army and navy commands.
4. *Defense Department Reorganization Act of 1958* strengthened Secretary of Defense's control of the three branches, centralized the Joint Chiefs of Staff, gave fuller budget controls to the Secretary of defense over the service branches.

II. THE JOINT CHIEFS OF STAFF

A. Who They Are

1. Serve as primary military advisers to the President, Secretary of Defense, National Security Council.
2. Five members are commanders of the four armed services and a chairman, all appointed by President with Senate approval.
3. Serve two-year terms for maximum of two terms.

B. What They Do

1. Advise and make recommendations to the civilian command.
2. Draft strategic plans.
3. Plan for supply and personnel needs of the services.
4. Provide U.S. military representation to international organizations.

C. Inter-Service Rivalries

1. Unification efforts have not terminated rivalries between the service branches.
2. Large part of rivalry today centers on role and function of service branches in nation's defense planning.

III. ARMS CONTROL

A. Advocates of Deterrence

1. East-West value conflict seen as cause of current U.S.-Soviet confrontation.
2. U.S. arms to match or surpass those of potential enemies viewed as best guarantee of peace.

B. Advocates of Disarmament or Arms Control

1. Agree that value conflict is major cause of international confrontation.
2. Hold that arsenal-building frightens other nations to build larger arsenals, and an unending spiral is created.
3. Argue that a too-large military poses a threat to democratic values at home.

C. Efforts at Arms Limitation

1. The United States, Russia, Great Britain began a voluntary ban on nuclear arms testing in 1958.
2. Voluntary 1958 nuclear test ban was honored for three years, when Russia resumed tests, while negotiations continued in Geneva for a test-ban treaty.
3. In 1963, the United States, Russia, Great Britain signed a treaty banning atmospheric tests of nuclear devices.
4. Two other nuclear powers, France and China, have continued to test nuclear weapons, unaffected by the three-party treaty.
5. U.S. and Soviet governments began *Strategic Arms Limitation (SALT)* talks at Helsinki in 1969, and these were continuing in May, 1972.

IV. IS ARMAMENT A NATURAL FOE OF DEMOCRACY?

A. U.S. Public Opinion

1. Reflects a historical civilian fear of the military.
2. Tends to resent large military expenditures, such as those occasioned by the Vietnam involvement, feeling that the money could better be spent at home.
3. Many Americans fear that large military spending creates a dire political force in the military-industrial complex which poses threat to basic democratic values.

B. Constitutional Precautions

1. Founding Fathers feared growth of arrogant, independent military.
2. Civilian command and control of military was their answer to the threat of military domination.
   a. President is Commander in Chief.
   b. All officers are commissioned by the President.
   c. Congress appropriates all moneys available for military spending.
   d. Military appropriations cannot exceed period of two years.
   e. Secretary of Defense and secretaries of service branches are required to be civilians.
   f. Congress bans military from controlling selection of candidates to service academies.

SELECTED TEST QUESTIONS

I. Multiple Choice

1. Members of the Joint Chiefs of Staff are named by the:
   (a) President; (b) Congress; (c) Secretary of Defense; (d) National Security Council.
2. In appropriating money for the military, the Constitution limits Congress to making outlays for:
   (a) one year; (b) two years; (c) three years; (d) four years.
3. The Unification Act of 1947 placed the sub-departments of army, navy, and air force under control of the:
   (a) Joint Chiefs of Staff; (b) Secretary of Defense; (c) Secretary of War; (d) Secretary of the Army.
4. The men who wrote the Constitution placed the military under civilian control because they thought:
   (a) civilians would know more about military affairs; (b) military officers would succeed to the presidency; (c) an independent military establishment could pose a threat to democratic values; (d) a civilian commander would be more aggressive in building the armed forces.
5. The only nation which has ever used nuclear weapons in warfare is:
   (a) Russia; (b) the United States; (c) China; (d) France.

II. True-False

1. The Unification Act of 1947 eliminated all rivalry among branches of the armed forces.
2. The Defense Department Reorganization Act of 1958 strengthened the role of the Secretary of Defense and advanced unification of the armed forces.
3. The Joint Chiefs of Staff are the principal military advisers to the President.
4. The Defense Department Reorganization Act of 1958 strengthened civilian control of the armed forces.
5. Only Congress may formally declare war, but the President may send troops abroad without a declaration of war.

CHAPTER 23

The Growing Function of Regulation

INTRODUCTION

Prior to the Great Depression of the 1930s American businessmen and industrialists operated under a bare minimum of regulation by the national government. State regulation and community regulation were common, but to a remarkably large degree, the business community operated in an aura of *laissez faire*—that is to say, subject only to its own self-imposed regulations.

Under such conditions, vast fortunes were amassed and tremendous commercial empires were established. Hard work and dedication, it was believed, could make a captain of industry of any man willing to subject himself to the discipline. To be sure, the muckrakers at the turn of the century had revealed that all is not gold which glitters in the American business community and among the barons of American industry. But money was the measure of success. If the muckrakers were so smart, why weren't they rich?

State regulation of some industries proved impractical. Railroads are a ready example. Rail commerce doesn't stop at state lines. Excesses in the nineteenth-century brand of *laissez-faire* enterprise brought demands for national regulations to control undesirable practices by business and industry.

Much of the early demand for governmental regulation of business was aimed at the ills which were believed to grow out of monopolistic business practices. In the late nineteenth century, it was believed that small businesses were victimized by the great monopolies in such products as oil, sugar, whiskey, and steel, for example.

Beginning in the second half of the nineteenth century, Congress found it necessary to establish "independent" regulatory agencies vested with authority to police broad areas of the American economy and regulate vast expanses of the American business community.

These regulatory agencies are independent from supervision by the President and oversight by heads of the regular Cabinet officers. Members of the regulatory commissions are appointed by the President with approval by the Senate. But the President may remove his appointees only for reasons stated by Congress in creating the respective agencies. In other words, these regulatory commissions form a branch of administrative apparatus which is relatively free of executive control. The status of such agencies in a democracy has caused much concern among scholars.

I. EARLY PROVISIONS FOR NATIONAL REGULATION OF BUSINESS

A. Interstate Commerce Commission (ICC)

1. First federal regulatory agency.
2. Created in 1887 by enactment of the *Interstate Commerce Act.*
3. Consists of 11 members appointed by President, with Senate approval, to serve seven-year terms.
4. Jurisdiction embraces interstate carriers, such as railroads, express companies, bus and truck companies, interstate oil pipelines, etc.
5. Responsible for fixing rates in interstate transportation.
6. Also has some authority over firms engaged in interstate transportation.

B. Sherman Antitrust Act

1. Passed by Congress in 1890.
2. Designed to encourage competition and stop growth of business monopolies.
3. Civil and criminal penalties prescribed for those employing business practices in restraint of interstate and foreign commerce.
4. Effectiveness was limited by Presidents' unenthusiastic enforcement.
5. Early Supreme Court decisions limited its effectiveness.
6. Enforcement responsibility placed in the Antitrust Division of the Department of Justice.

C. Clayton Act

1. Passed by Congress in 1914 as a major antitrust act aimed at increasing competition in business.
2. Forbids price cutting and other practices which may destroy competition.
3. Restricts stock and ownership transfers and interlocking directorates which might result in reduced competition.
4. Nonprofit labor unions and agricultural organizations are exempted from provisions.
5. Intended to strengthen provisions of the Sherman Act, which had been undercut by the Supreme Court.
6. Enforcement has been weakened through administrative apathy and judicial tolerance.
7. Enforcement responsibility rests with Antitrust Division of Justice Department and with Federal Trade Commission.

D. Federal Trade Commission

1. Established by Congress in 1914 to enforce the Clayton Act and the Federal Trade Commission Act of 1914.
2. Five members appointed by President with Senate approval.
3. Members serve seven-year terms.
4. Main job is to promote fair competition in business and restrict unfair business practices in interstate and foreign commerce.
5. Seeks to prevent illegal combinations in restraint of trade, deceptive advertising, price discrimination, price fixing, interlocking directorates, and other business practices which might reduce competition or defraud consumers.
6. Makes rules and establishes codes of fair competition.
7. Holds hearings and may use cease-and-desist order to force compliance.
8. Greatest effort is directed toward protecting consumer interests by preventing deceptive advertising, fraud, and sale of dangerous products.
9. Sometimes viewed as the national government's greatest effort toward maintaining the private enterprise system by preventing corrupt practices.

II. GOVERNMENT REGULATION AND THE DEPRESSION

A. Public Opinion Toward Business

1. Economic collapse revealed much corruption in American business system.
2. Public opinion turned against *laissez-faire* business enterprise.
3. Business reforms were demanded.

B. Business and the New Deal

1. Franklin D. Roosevelt tried to revive stagnated business activity by suspending enforcement of antitrust legislation through the *National Industrial Recovery Act (NIRA)*.
2. New emphasis on enforcement of antitrust laws began in 1938.

3. Supreme Court, prior to 1937 opposed to regulation of business by national government, has since found regulation more acceptable.
4. Since 1930s Justice Department has been generally vigorous in enforcing antitrust laws.

III. CONCENTRATION OF ECONOMIC POWER

A. Scope of Concentration

1. Five hundred largest American corporations own more than two-thirds of nation's manufacturing assets.
2. Two thousand corporations worth more than $10 million each process 80 percent of all resources used in manufacturing.
3. Conglomerate ownership of industry continues on upswing.
4. Consolidation of banking control appears as trend.

B. Critics and Remedies

1. *John K. Galbraith,* Harvard economist, questions effectiveness of federal antitrust regulation, saying that it does not strike at the heart of oligopoly—the real core of concentration of economic power.
2. *Ralph Nadar* is one of many critics of federal antitrust enforcement.
3. Nadar proposes FTC and Antitrust Division of Justice Department be consolidated in new agency, with tenfold budget increase, with penalties for antitrust violations increased.
4. Antitrust Division of Justice Department has recommended increase in criminal penalties for corporations, but congressional approval has been withheld.

C. Two Views of Giants in Business

1. Ralph Nadar's objections.
   a. Bigness should be outlawed.
   b. Giant corporations should be broken up by government.
   c. Bigness stifles competition.
   d. Bigness works against interests of consumers.
2. David Lilienthal's defense.
   a. Big business more efficient.
   b. Promotes national security.
   c. Promotes freedom and individualism.
   d. Stimulates competition.
   e. Fosters more research.
   f. Markets better products.
   g. Maintains better labor-management relations.
   h. Creates stability of employment.
   i. Increases production.
   j. Promotes conservation.
   k. Increases opportunities for small businessmen.

D. Consumer Protection Agencies

1. *Federal Trade Commission.*
   a. In recent years, has turned increasingly toward representing consumer interests in regulation of business.
   b. Funds appropriated by Congress allow only token effort on behalf of American consumers.

2. Office of Consumer Affairs in the Executive Office of the President.
3. Consumer Protection Section, Antitrust Division, Department of Justice.
4. *Food and Drug Administration,* Department of Health, Education and Welfare.
5. *Federal Communications Commission.*
6. Many other regulatory agencies are at least indirectly interested in protecting consumer interests.

E. Environmental Protection Efforts

1. Only in recent years has emphasis been placed on protection of the natural environment against spoliation by industry and individuals.
2. Until recently considered a problem to be dealt with mainly by the states, environmental protection has now come within the expanding area of interest of the national government.
3. Two federal environmental agencies.
   a. *Council on Environmental Quality.*
      (1) Part of the Executive Office of the President.
      (2) Originates and recommends environmental laws to the President and to Congress.
   b. *Environmental Protection Agency.*
      (1) Independent agency responsible to the President.
      (2) Responsible for enforcement of federal laws for protection of the environment.
4. Two recent federal anti-pollution laws.
   a. *Air Pollution Act of 1970.*
      (1) Sets health standards of air, water, etc.
      (2) Grants research funds to states, localities.
      (3) Sponsored controversial 1975 deadline for improvement of automobile exhaust systems.
   b. *Water Quality Improvement Act of 1970.*
      (1) Undertakes to make polluters responsible for cleanup.
      (2) Encourages greater investment by states and cities for improved water control and sewage treatment.

IV. NATIONAL GOVERNMENT AND LABOR-MANAGEMENT RELATIONS

A. Historical Perspective

1. Earliest efforts to organize American workers were bitterly opposed by businessmen and industrial leaders.
2. Property-oriented state courts were effective in blocking many organizing efforts.
3. Clamor for reform produced many state laws recognizing legality of trade unions.
4. Many employers adopted "yellow-dog" contracts, by which new employees pledged not to join labor union.
5. Courts so narrowly interpreted state laws as to weaken legal status of unions.
6. Injunctions were often used by employers to end strikes and block picketing.
7. U.S. Supreme Court's hostility toward organized labor was reflected in its opinions.
8. National government led the way in improving conditions for workingmen.
   a. In 1840, Congress established ten-hour day in navy yards.
   b. Congress established eight-hour day for railroad employees and seamen.

B. Federal Efforts to Protect Workers

1. *Norris-LaGuardia Act of 1932.*
   a. Outlawed "yellow-dog" contracts by which workers were required to agree not to join unions.

    b. Limited use of injunction, which had become a common weapon of management against labor.

    c. One of the first national laws favoring organized labor.

2. *National Industrial Recovery Act of 1933*

    a. Section 7a contained first federal guarantee of right of workers to organize.

    b. Banned employer interference with right of workers to organize.

    c. Declared unconstitutional by U.S. Supreme Court in 1935.

3. *National Labor Relations Act of 1935 (Wagner Act)*

    a. Resurrected Section 7a of NRA.

    b. Guaranteed right of labor to organize and bargain collectively.

    c. Barred employer interference with right of workers to organize and bargain collectively.

    d. Established the *National Labor Relations Board (NLRB)* to administer the act.

    e. Authorized the NLRB to issue cease-and-desist orders to employers who commit unfair practices, as defined by the act.

    f. Remained in force until 1947.

    g. Was instrumental in building labor-union membership from four to fifteen million.

    h. Helped win acceptance of union contracts by great majority of U.S. manufacturing plants.

4. *Walsh-Healey Act of 1936.*

    a. Required payment of prevailing wages by firms contracting with national government.

    b. Required overtime payment for work exceeding eight hours a day or 40 hours a week.

    c. Banned used of convict labor or child labor on government contracts.

5. *Fair Labor Standards Act of 1938*

    a. Set maximum work week of 40 hours for employees engaged in interstate commerce or making goods shipped in interstate commerce.

    b. Set minimum wage at 25 cents an hour and required time-and-a-half for work exceeding 40 hours a week.

6. *Occupational Safety and Health Act of 1970*

    a. Created first broad federal industrial safety program.

    b. Authorizes Secretary of Labor to establish health and safety standards for workers in companies in interstate commerce.

C. Controversial Labor Practices

1. *Featherbedding* developed as a means of preventing layoffs resulting from development of labor-saving devices.

2. Closed shop—a labor-management contract which provides that only union members may be hired.

3. Some corruption developed in union leadership and was widely publicized.

4. A few unions were infiltrated by Communists at a time when the nation was very frightened of the *red menace.*

5. Some unions abandoned democratic principles, and leaders ruled them with autocratic hand.

D. Labor-Management Relations Act of 1947 (Taft-Hartley Act)

1. Enacted in response to a belief that labor unions had become too strong.

2. Bitterly opposed by labor unions.

3. Sought to equalize relative powers of employers and labor unions.

4. Imposed limitations on labor union practices.

5. Sought to strengthen the position of individual worker.

6. Outlawed the closed shop, jurisdictional strikes, secondary boycotts, political expenditures by unions, excessive dues.

7. Permits use of injunction and "cooling off" practices in strikes which threaten the national welfare.
8. Placed accounting responsibilities on union leaders.
9. Act passed over President Truman's veto by Republican-controlled Congress.
10. Permitted employers and unions to sue each other in federal courts for contract violations.
11. Made it unfair labor practice for union to refuse to bargain with employer.

E. Labor-Reform Act of 1959 (Landrum-Griffin Act)

1. Strengthens Taft-Hartley Act restrictions on internal procedures of labor unions.
2. Provides "bill of rights" for union members.
3. Requires detailed financial reports by unions to the Secretary of Labor.
4. Makes misuse of union funds a federal crime.
5. Bars ex-convicts, Communists, and persons with conflicting interests from holding union office.
6. Requires secret elections for local union officers at least once every three years and for national officers at least once every five years.

V. FEDERAL MACHINERY FOR PRESERVING LABOR-MANAGEMENT PEACE

A. National Labor Relations Board

1. Created by the Wagner Act of 1935.
2. Independent regulatory commission which administers the Wagner Act and the Taft-Hartley Act as they relate to unfair labor practices and the designation of bargaining agents.
3. Five members appointed by President with Senate approval to serve five-year terms.
4. Authorized to issue cease-and-desist orders, hold impartial elections for bargaining representatives, and to utilize federal courts for enforcement of its orders.

B. Federal Mediation and Conciliation Service

1. Headed by director appointed by President with Senate consent.
2. Helps settle labor-management disputes in industries affecting interstate commerce, except for railroads and airlines.
3. May enter dispute on request by one of parties or when substantial interruption of interstate commerce is threatened.
4. Professional mediators try to promote good relations between labor and management.
5. Operates as independent agency outside Department of Labor.
6. Has no law-enforcement authority, but relies on persuasion.

C. National Mediation Board

1. Established in 1934 as independent agency in national government.
2. Responsible for mediating labor-management differences in railroad and airline transportation industries.
3. Three members appointed by President with Senate approval.
4. Can determine bargaining representatives for workers.
5. President may place carriers under government operation if mediation efforts fail.

D. Taft-Hartley Act Enforcement

1. When a major labor-management dispute threatens national health or safety, the President may appoint a special fact-finding board.
2. President is authorized to direct the Attorney General to seek an 80-day injunction to postpone a strike.

3. If the court agrees that the national health or safety is threatened, injunction is issued.

4. If dispute remains unsettled after 80 days, the board informs President of employer's last offer for settlement.

5. The NLRB conducts secret ballot among employees to determine if offer is acceptable.

6. If dispute remains unsettled, President reports to Congress with his recommendation, and workers may proceed with strike.

VI. NATURE OF INDEPENDENT REGULATORY COMMISSIONS

A. Functions

1. Executive.
2. Judicial.
3. Legislative.

B. Status in Federal Bureaucracy

1. Independent of control by President.
2. Organized outside 11 major Cabinet departments.

C. Reasons for Independence

1. Free of presidential politics.
2. Adjudicatory function free of executive supervision.
3. Commissioners viewed as specialists, dealing with technical subjects.

D. Two Major Criticisms

1. Independent commissions are beyond the pale of democratic theory, not necessarily responsive to public opinion.
2. Clientele industries often come into control of commissions which are supposed to regulate their activities: the regulators are regulated by the regulatees.

SELECTED TEST QUESTIONS

I. Multiple Choice

1. The first independent regulatory commission was:
   (a) the Interstate Commerce Commission; (b) Federal Trade Commission; (c) Securities and Exchange Commission; (d) Federal Power Commission.

2. The independent regulatory commission created to police competitive business practices, but increasingly interested in consumer protection is the:
   (a) Interstate Commerce Commission; (b) Federal Trade Commission; (c) Federal Power Commission; (d) Securities and Exchange Commission.

3. The national law which first outlawed the "yellow-dog" contract and recognized the right of workers to organize and bargain collectively was the:
   (a) Taft-Hartley Act; (b) Wagner Act; (c) Norris-LaGuardia Act; (d) Landrum-Griffin Act.

4. The National Labor Relations Board was created to administer the:
   (a) Norris-LaGuardia Act; (b) Wagner Act; (c) Taft-Hartley Act; (d) Landrum-Griffin Act.

5. In national legislation, the closed shop was outlawed by:
   (a) the Norris-LaGuardia Act; (b) the Wagner Act; (c) the Fair Labor Standards Act; (d) the Taft-Hartley Act.

II. True-False

1. The Taft-Hartley Act was passed by Congress over President Truman's veto.
2. The Wagner Act was instrumental in building the power and membership of labor unions.
3. Organized labor strongly supported adoption of the Taft-Hartley Act.
4. U.S. businessmen in general reacted favorably to provisions of the Wagner Act.
5. The NLRB has power only to make recommendations in labor-management disputes.

CHAPTER 24

What the Government Promotes

INTRODUCTION

In some parts of the country, and in some social groups, lively and heated discussion surrounds the subject of government subsidization for various elements of the economy. Targets of criticism change with time and place. Thus on the plains of West Texas, where the remnants of a rugged individualism still persist, one can find much criticism of the government's relatively new welfare "give-away" programs such as unemployment compensation and aid to the families of dependent children.

The values of many on what is left of the American frontier would seem to hold strongly that if a man doesn't work, he shouldn't eat and that parents who cannot support children shouldn't have them in the first place. These values are part of what John Galbraith, Harvard economist, has described as "conventional wisdom" in some parts of rural America. At the same time, rural dwellers who hold these values may be altogether uncritical of the various federal programs aimed at the regulation and subsidization of agriculture. Similarly, businessmen may be quite critical of agriculture-subsidy programs and totally oblivious to the fact that the oldest subsidy programs operated by the national government are for the direct benefit of some American business.

It is doubtful that any person reaches maturity in the United States today without having benefited from a number of programs which draw support directly from some agency of government—national, state, or local.

Direct and indirect subsidies by the national government for the encouragement of desirable ends are as old as the nation itself. One congressional committee, in defending agricultural incentives, has reported that the first law passed by the first Congress of the United States provided a subsidy for the infant American maritime interests.

Protective tariffs for American industry are as old as the nation itself. It is, of course, in the interest of the entire nation that America have a healthy business community. Education was benefiting from national subsidies even before the Constitution was written. Other federal subsidy programs have embraced agriculture, health, science, and economically deprived persons.

I. NATIONAL GOVERNMENT AIDS TO BUSINESS

A. Maintaining Economic Stability

1. Protection of property.
2. Enforcement of contracts.
3. Business-oriented monetary policy.

B. Aids to Business in International Trade

1. Tariffs.
   a. Revenue source characteristic of young nations.
   b. Originated early in U.S. history to protect infant industry against "dumping" by British manufacturers.
   c. Raises price of imports and benefits domestic producers.
   d. Of declining importance in recent years, but revival of protectionist spirit has been noted.

2. Import quotas
3. Minimum prices on imports.
4. Import prohibitions.

II. NATIONAL GOVERNMENT AIDS TO AGRICULTURE

A. The "Farm Problem"

1. Trend toward consolidation.
   a. Family farms decreasing in number.
   b. Advantages of technology accrue mainly to large farm operations.
   c. Increased output means lower unit prices, thus placing severe economic squeeze on small farmers.
2. Social imbalance.
   a. Social and economic advances often do not reach rural communities.
   b. Common services—like education, sanitation, and fire protection—are often inadequate in rural America.
   c. Substandard housing commoner in rural America than in cities.
   d. One-skill nature of farming disadvantages many who migrate to the cities.
3. Economic dilemma.
   a. Production has increased faster than demand, resulting in deflated commodity prices.
   b. Technological advances have led to higher capital investment and often increased production costs not reflected in increased commodity prices.

B. Areas of Government Aid

1. Conservation assistance.
2. Cooperative organization assistance.
3. Credit incentives.
4. Research.
5. Agricultural education.
6. Production and marketing controls.
   a. Acreage allotments to prevent commodity surpluses.
   b. Marketing quotas to discourage "glut" on market.
   c. Conservation payments to reduce acres in production.
7. Market incentives.
   a. Credit and currency provisions for overseas sales of surplus commodities.
   b. Food stamp program for the needy.
   c. School lunch program.
   d. School milk program.

III. NATIONAL GOVERNMENT PROMOTION OF SCIENCE

A. Constitutional Provisions

1. Authorization of the national census.
2. Provision for standard weights and measures.
3. Authorization for protection of inventors through patent provision.

B. Science-Related Agencies

1. *National Science Foundation*
   a. Director appointed by President with Senate approval.

b. Twenty-four-man board of scientists.

c. Grants matching funds for facilities and fellowships.

d. Grants funds to support thousands of scientific studies.

2. *National Institutes of Health.*

a. Agency of National Health Services.

b. Grant program supports health sciences.

c. In addition to supporting nongovernmental studies, operates own research programs and hospitals.

3. *Atomic Energy Commission.*

a. Five commissioners appointed by President with Senate approval.

b. Oversees and fosters research and development of atomic energy.

c. Regulates all private efforts in atomic energy field.

d. Primarily interested in development and stockpiling of atomic weapons.

e. Work supervised by Congress through its Joint Committee on Atomic Energy.

IV. FEDERAL ASSISTANCE TO THE NEEDY

A. Historical Perspective

1. Aid to the needy administered by churches for centuries.

2. In early U.S. history, counties and other local governments administered aid to widows and orphans.

3. State governments later helped with laws favoring needy persons.

4. Great Depression was turning point. State and local governments, unable to finance the broad programs needed, watched the national government expand its public welfare activities.

5. The depression-born "emergency relief program" has expanded into a broad, many-faceted federal welfare program.

6. Although the national government supplies much of the money, programs are generally administered by state and local governments.

7. More than 13 million Americans benefit from government welfare programs today, with many more needing assistance.

B. Major Classes of Beneficiaries

1. Unemployed.

2. Aged.

3. Physically handicapped.

4. Dependent children.

C. Three Approaches to Ending the Need for Welfare Assistance

1. President Franklin D. Roosevelt advocated full employment as solution.

2. In the 1960s, the emphasis was on providing professional services to the needy—in a sense, reordering their lives.

3. President Lyndon Johnson's War on Poverty emphasized organizing the needy into political action groups.

V. SOCIAL INSURANCE PROGRAMS

A. Characteristics

1. Administered on basis of legal right, rather than need.

2. Major provisions based on *Social Security Act of 1935.*

3. Least controversial of federal welfare programs, because benefits are "earned."

B. Programs

    1. Unemployment insurance.
       a. Provides payments for limited time to workers unemployed for reasons beyond their control.
       b. Administered by states under national supervision.
       c. Financed by payroll tax on employers of four or more workers.
       d. 62 million workers covered by some kind of unemployment insurance.
       e. Benefits vary from state to state.
       f. Major groups lacking in coverage are farm workers, domestics, and state and local government employees.
    2. Old age, survivors', disability, and Medicare insurance.
       a. Employers and employees contribute fixed rates.
       b. Pays monthly benefits to persons sixty-two years of age and older.
       c. Size of benefits based on worker's contributions and number of persons entitled to secondary benefits.
       d. Disabled workers may retire and draw benefits at any age.
       e. Law limits amount person may earn while drawing benefits between ages of sixty-two and seventy-two.
       f. Benefits also provided for survivors.
       g. Medicare program, enacted in 1965, provides medical benefits for persons past sixty-five years of age.
          (1) Provides hospital payments, nursing-home care, some home nursing and outpatient services.
          (2) Funds collected and administered separately from other Social Security taxes.
          (3) Two million persons not covered by other Social Security provisions included in Medicare, with funds drawn from general revenue.
          (4) Supplemental benefits available for payment of small fee.

VI. WELFARE PROGRAMS

A. General Perspective

    1. National government made large grants to states during Great Depression to make welfare payments to needy persons.
    2. Originally viewed as temporary venture by national government, federal aid has never been abandoned.
    3. Welfare provisions viewed as permanent need in American society.
    4. States retain primary responsibility for welfare.
    5. In contrast to social insurance programs, public assistance, or welfare, programs were designed to give immediate and continuing assistance to the needy.

B. Old-Age Assistance

    1. Enacted to help those at or near retirement age at time of passage of Social Security Act of 1935.
    2. Need for program was expected to disappear as younger persons qualified for social insurance benefits.
    3. Independently of national government, 25 states had established such programs by 1935.
    4. Aid is extended on basis of need, beginning at age sixty-five.
    5. States pay part of costs of program.
    6. Amount of assistance varies from $10 to $90 a month among the states.
    7. Ten percent of all persons over sixty-five in the United States receive aid.

C. Aid to the Blind

1. National program of assistance to blind also started in 1935.
2. Available to persons at age of sixteen or eighteen, depending on school status, whose eyesight deficiencies incapacitate them for normal employment.
3. Program administered by states with financial help from national government.
4. One-third of blind persons in the United States receive assistance, which averages $88 a month each.

D. Aid to Families of Dependent Children

1. Federal participation in programs started in 1935.
2. Several states had aid programs before 1935.
3. Basic aim is to make it possible for needy families to stay together.
4. Most controversial of public assistance programs.
5. Eligibility extends to one under eighteen, who has been deprived of parental support, but who is living with other parent or other close relative; also to families in which both parents are unemployed.
6. Program helps five million children, two million mothers, and 200,000 fathers.
7. Able parents are encouraged to work, and Congress has provided day-care centers.

E. Aid to Totally and Permanently Disabled

1. National grants first made available in 1950.
2. Benefits available to persons eighteen and over who are totally and permanently disabled, but not mentally ill or tubercular.
3. In 1968, 635,000 persons received grants averaging $88 a month.
4. National government pays more than half of cost of program.

VII. OFFICE OF ECONOMIC OPPORTUNITY

A. Origin

1. Created by *Economic Opportunity Act of 1964* as major thrust of President Lyndon Johnson's "war on poverty."
2. Part of the Executive Office of the President.
3. Coordinating center for distributing funds to other agencies and operates own poverty programs.
4. Stresses education and training in an effort to reach causes of poverty.

B. Three OEO Programs

1. *Operation Headstart.*
   a. School-orientation program for disadvantaged preschoolers.
   b. Aimed at counteracting handicap children from needy homes often have on entering school.
2. *Neighborhood Youth Corps.*
   a. Provides out-of-school job training.
   b. Aimed at teenagers who have dropped out, or are about to drop out, of high school.
3. *Community Action Program.*
   a. Intended to stimulate communities to organize their own resources against poverty.
   b. Most controversial of "war-on-poverty" programs.
   c. Directed toward unifying fragmented communities of disadvantaged persons.

VIII. HOUSING AND URBAN DEVELOPMENT

A. Assistance in Housing

1. National government has had public housing program since 1937.
2. Federal Housing Administration's mortgage insurance has encouraged home ownership by low-income and middle-income families.
3. Public housing program has created 650,000 dwellings for 2.5 million people.
4. Recent development in housing assistance has been rent subsidies for the poor.

B. Assistance in Urban Development

1. Federal funds for urban renewal encourage city slum-clearance projects.
2. Funds also available for improvement of municipal services, such as mass transit and sewage systems.
3. *Model Cities Act of 1968* made federal funds available for coordinated programs to improve areas within cities.
4. Six million units of low-income housing a year was the goal of the 1960 *Housing and Urban Development Act*, which provides subsidies for mortgages and rent payments.

IX. CHILD HEALTH AND WELFARE

A. Historical Perspective

1. National government briefly aided state programs of maternity care and child welfare in the 1920s.
2. Social Security Act of 1935 established child health and welfare service program.
3. Headstart Program, enacted in 1964, attempted to bridge gap between home and school for children in disadvantaged families.

B. Administration

1. Under Social Security Act, grants-in-aid are made to states and territories for support of state activities.
2. Grants correspond to demonstrated need and must be spent according to federal guidelines.
3. Helps county health departments maintain health services for children from birth through school age, for mothers before and after childbirth.

SELECTED TEST QUESTIONS

I. Multiple Choice

1. The first private interest group in the United States to receive general economic assistance from the national government was:
   (a) business; (b) agriculture; (c) labor; (d) the needy.
2. A revenue source characteristic of young nations is the:
   (a) sales tax; (b) income tax; (c) property tax; (d) tariffs.
3. An expansion of welfare activities by the federal government was noted during:
   (a) the Civil War; (b) the second half of the nineteenth century; (c) World War I; (d) the Great Depression.
4. The national government first assumed a massive interest in farm prosperity during:
   (a) the Civil War; (b) World War I; (c) World War II; (d) the Great Depression.

5. Those parts of the national welfare system which people participate in as a matter of right, rather than need, are often referred to as:
(a) public assistance; (b) social insurance; (c) public welfare; (d) the war on poverty.

II. True-False

1. Aid to the needy is a responsibility which has shifted from the national government to state and local governments in recent years.
2. Aid to Families of Dependent Children is a part of the American program of social insurance.
3. An unemployed worker must prove he is needy before he can draw unemployment compensation.
4. During the Great Depression, the national government entered the public welfare field after the states generally had shown no interest.
5. Operation Headstart was designed as a preschool program for disadvantaged children.

CHAPTER 25

Managing Government Operations

INTRODUCTION

Entrenched economic individualists have long maintained that government should stay out of business. In recent decades, most have acknowledged that governmental *regulation* of businesses vested with a public interest — such as transportation and public utilities — is acceptable. But many will wave the red flag of socialism at the suggestion of government *ownership and operation* of business enterprises.

A world tide of pragmatic necessity has been running against such advocates of economic individualism for many decades. From the very beginning of the national history of the United States, the national government has taken an interest in the direct management of some enterprises — for example, the postal service — and state governments have long been directly interested in the management of others — for example, public education.

The worldwide trend — especially in the past three decades — has been for government to take direct interest in the management of more and more enterprises. This trend has been less apparent in the United States than in many other democratic nations — such as Australia, Britain, and Sweden — but it has been nonetheless an unmistakable trend.

Public ownership of the instruments of production is one definition of socialism. Americans would seem to be willing to accept the practice while rejecting the name.

The greatest incentive to government ownership and management came with the economic distress of the Great Depression in the decade of the 1930s. Then it was discovered that the private interprise system did not work according to its basic theory. With business driven to the wall, many economic individualists even advocated government ownership and operation of businesses said to be the cornerstone of a capitalist economy. How difficult it is today to believe that some bankers in that tragic period of history favored a takeover of the nation's banking by the national government.

The national government did not take over the banking system. It did create institutions such as the Federal Deposit Insurance Corporation to guarantee security in savings to the American people. But the national government did expand into many fields of enterprise which had theretofore been considered off limits for government.

Americans are noted for the practical approach they take to problem-solving. It would be difficult to say that the nation has any *policy* on the subject of public versus private ownership or management. In time of unlimited warfare, few Americans question the necessity for the national government to assume control of practically the entire business and industrial life of the nation. If the President assumes control of the nation's railroads and other public carriers, few questions are asked. But it is expected that private control will be resumed after the emergency has passed.

In normal times, however, the extent of government intrusion into the realm of private enterprise can become a burning question. A major point made by those who oppose government ownership and management of across-the-counter enterprises is based on a fear of governmental size.

Big government, they say, poses a threat to individual liberties. This is often branded a "conservative" argument. President Harry Truman once declared that big government is necessary to protect individual liberties.

I. THE PUBLIC-PRIVATE POLICY DILEMMA

A. Examples of Enterprises Operated by National Government

1. Armed forces.
2. Postal Service.
3. Hospitals.
4. Parks.
5. Insurance.
6. Power generating facilities.
7. Dams and lakes.
8. U.S. Government Printing Office.

B. Characteristics of Government-Operated Enterprises

1. Not inspired by profit motive.
2. Many essential for general welfare and unity of nation.
3. Many directed toward security and convenience of citizens.
4. Some incidental to traditional functions of government.
5. Some essential to efficient governmental operation in general.

C. Some Arguments Against Government Operation

1. With unlimited resources, government cannot operate on equal basis in competition with private enterprise.
2. Unfair to use taxpayer's money to compete with him in business.
3. Political control of business-type management cannot be efficient.
4. Enterprise-management promotes governmental growth, and big government poses threat to individual liberties.
5. Enterprise operated without profit motive must be inefficient.
6. All enterprises operated by national government lose money—proof of inefficiency.

D. Some Arguments Favoring Government Operation

1. Some enterprises are so basically necessary for public welfare that they should be provided without profit motive.
2. Some enterprises are inherently profitless, but are needed for public welfare.
3. Some enterprises involve such great capital investment as to be beyond the reach of private enterprisers.
4. Some enterprises are of such a nature that their management and availability must be responsive to political pressures.

II. DELIVERING THE MAIL

A. Historical Sketch

1. Post office was established under colonial rule.
   a. Benjamin Franklin served two decades as British Postmaster General for colonies.
   b. Franklin was to remain head of post office for newly independent states for two years during the American Revolution.
2. Congress was authorized to "establish Post Offices and Post Roads" by Article I of the Constitution.

B. United States Post Office Department

1. Accorded Cabinet rank in 1829.
2. Cabinet post of Postmaster General for many years remained hub of political activity and patronage in succeeding administrations, with many jobs for party faithful.
3. National chairman of incoming President's political party was commonly named Postmaster General.
4. Inefficiency and corruption were common for many years.
5. Civil Service reforms gradually removed most employees from patronage control.

C. United States Postal Service

1. Created by Congress in 1970 as an independent agency to carry on the work of the abolished Post Office Department.
2. Change followed lengthy study and debate.
3. Transition toward self-supporting business enterprise started in 1971.
4. Controlled by 11-member Board of Governors.
   a. Nine appointed by President with Senate approval to serve staggered nine-year terms.
   b. No more than five of presidential appointees may be of one political party.
   c. Nine appointed members appoint Postmaster General, who also serves as a tenth board member.
   d. Ten board members name a Deputy Postmaster General, who serves as eleventh board member.
5. Employees retain civil service status.
6. Tax revenues will continue to support Postal Service during transition to self-supporting enterprise.
7. Organizational structure is intended to assure recognition of service responsibility of Postal Service.

III. TENNESSEE VALLEY AUTHORITY

A. Historical Sketch

1. To produce nitrogen for explosives during World War I, the national government bought hydro-electric generating facilities at Muscle Shoals on the Tennessee River.
2. After the war, Senator George W. Norris, Nebraska Republican, launched a drive to involve the national government in development of the entire Tennessee Valley.
3. After long debate, Congress in 1933 created the Tennessee Valley Authority, a government corporation, to carry out a broad development program.
4. TVA responsibilities included improving river navigability, flood control, reforestation, agricultural and industrial development, and strengthening the national defense.
5. TVA, it was hoped, would improve economic and social conditions of people in 40,000-square-mile area.
6. TVA was loudly denounced as a socialistic innovation.

B. Tennessee Valley Authority Today

1. Commonly hailed as a notable success.
2. Corporation operates under board of three directors appointed by President with Senate approval.
3. Operations extend into seven states.
4. Almost 30 major dams have been built and others are planned.

5. Tennessee River flooding has been arrested.
6. Produces vast quantities of electricity.
7. Navigation and agriculture have been improved.
8. Manufactures and sells fertilizers.
9. Water pollution and malaria infection have been reduced.
10. Source of low-cost electricity has attracted industry, created employment opportunities.
11. Recreational facilities have been built.

IV. ATOMIC ENERGY COMMISSION (AEC)

A. Historical Sketch

1. Crash program of atomic research conducted in secrecy during World War II.
2. Major objective was to create devastating new weapon.
3. Success of research was announced to world with use of atomic bombs in 1945 to hasten Japanese surrender.
4. New discovery and its control led to major public debate throughout nation.
5. Energy of atom increasingly recognized as major new source of non-military power.

B. Major Policy Questions Raised

1. Would atomic energy remain under government control or be turned over to private interests for exploitation?
2. If government retained control, should supervision be military or civilian?

C. Atomic Energy Acts of 1946, 1954

1. Act of 1946 created civilian-controlled AEC to control and develop uses of atomic energy under governmental supervision.
2. Commission established as independent agency responsible for stimulating research and development of atomic energy and regulating all private efforts in field.
3. Commission consists of five members appointed by President with Senate approval to serve five-year terms.
4. Act of 1954 seeks to involve private enterprise to greater degree in exploitation of atomic energy.
5. With large government subsidies, major research effort is directed toward use of atomic energy in production of electric power.

V. RAISING THE MONEY FOR NATIONAL GOVERNMENT OPERATION

A. Historical Sketch

1. Articles of Confederation gave Congress no authority to tax.
2. U.S. Constitution of 1787 authorized Congress" to lay and collect taxes, duties, imposts, and excises," thus creating what was to become one of the greatest powers of Congress.
3. Three limitations on taxing power.
   a. Duties and excise taxes must be levied uniformly throughout the United States.
   b. Direct taxes had to be apportioned among the states according to population (changed by sixteenth amendment).
   c. No tax is to be levied on exports from any state.
4. Greatest source of federal revenue during most of nineteenth century was tariff.
5. Excise taxes on manufacture or sale of certain products also figured as prominent revenue source, as it does today.

6. Federal tax on incomes was levied briefly during Civil War and again in 1894, but was declared unconstitutional by U.S. Supreme Court in 1895.
7. Sixteenth amendment, ratified in 1915, authorized Congress to levy income tax, which has since become the greatest single source of revenue for the national government.

B. Major Sources of National Tax Revenues

1. Individual income tax.
   a. Produces more than 40 percent of national tax revenue.
   b. Original low rate has been increased, especially during times of war.
   c. Originally affected few persons, but has been broadly expanded to tax vast majority of wage earners.
   d. Based on graduated scale, with higher rate on larger incomes, in effort to tax according to ability to pay.
   e. Major advantage is flexibility as tool for regulating national economy.
   f. Major disadvantage is complexity, which has caused much criticism and encouraged some questionable avoidance.
2. Corporation income taxes.
   a. Raise about 16 percent of national tax revenue.
   b. Formerly yielded largest share of federal tax revenue.
3. Excise taxes.
   a. Some earmarked for specific purposes.
   b. Major excises not earmarked are collected on liquor, tobacco, air travel, and other purported "luxury" goods and services.
   c. Some excise taxes were first levied during World War II, but were not reduced or eliminated until 1965; others are being slowly reduced.
   d. Currently account for 8 percent of federal tax revenue.
4. Customs duties.
   a. Once constituted the main source of federal tax revenue.
   b. Today yields about $500 million a year.

C. Evaluation of Specific Taxes

1. Graduated income tax.
   a. Easy to collect.
   b. Taxes according to ability to pay.
2. Excise taxes.
   a. As used by national government, apply mainly to "luxury" items, are thus related to ability to pay.
   b. May be selectively applied so as to influence private spending.
   c. May be used to discourage spending, thus serving as tool for regulation of national economy.
   d. More expensive to collect than income tax.
3. General sales tax.
   a. Considered *regressive* in that it may not be related to ability to pay.
   b. On July 1, 1971, the U.S. Treasury Department listed 45 states which collected sales taxes in various forms.
   c. Claimed by proponents as deterrent to inflation.

D. Tax Bills in Congress

1. Constitution provides all revenue measures must originate in House of Representatives.
   a. This provision has caused much friction between House and Senate.
   b. House Ways and Means Committee handles tax proposals for House of Representatives.

2. President usually has much influence on tax measures, since he initiates the budget.

3. Strong contention over major tax measures is common, as various interest groups seek to shift tax burden.

VI. SPENDING ON THE NATIONAL GOVERNMENT

A. Handling the Money

1. All federal revenues and expenditures are handled at one point by the Treasury Department.
   a. *Internal Revenue Service*, a Treasury unit, handles most tax collections.
   b. *Bureau of Customs* collects customs duties.
2. *Comptroller General* has authority to approve all expenditures.

B. The Federal Budget

1. President is responsible for formulating national budget under the *Budget and Accounting Act of 1921*.
2. Formulation begins with estimates of expenditures.
3. *Office of Management and Budget* screens and prunes budget requests, often calling on agencies to justify estimates and programs.
4. In consultation with the President, Budget Director prepares proposed unified budget.
5. President presents budget to Congress, pointing out major areas of change and emphasis.
6. Congress holds hearings on the President's proposed budget and is free to make alterations.

C. Checking on Expenditures

1. *General Accounting Office*, headed by Comptroller General, is responsible for validating and auditing expenditures.
   a. *Comptroller General* appointed by President with Senate approval to serve 15-year term.
   b. Office originally viewed as agency of Congress to check on administration, so is not responsible to the President.

VII. NATIONAL MONEY MANAGEMENT

A. The Money

1. Under the Articles of Confederation, Congress issued currency which became worthless.
2. Constitution gives Congress power to manage U.S. monetary system.
3. Before Constitution was adopted, states issued own separate currencies.
4. Constitution expressly gave Congress power to coin money, regulate its value; states were barred from issuing currency.

B. Banks and Banking

1. All commercial banks in the United States are privately owned.
2. Banks are subject to government supervision.
3. Of 14,000 banks in the United States, 4,800 are chartered by national government.
4. Most state banks, like the national banks, are subject to federal regulation because their accounts are insured by the Federal Deposit Insurance Corporation.
5. *Federal Deposit Insurance Corporation, (FDIC)*, established by Congress in 1933, insures deposits in member banks up to $20,000.
6. *Federal Savings and Loan Insurance Corporation (FSLIC)* protects deposits in member institutions up to $20,000.

C. Federal Reserve System

1. Private-public banking agency created by Congress in 1913.
2. Intended to regulate banking policies and influence the amount of credit available and currency in circulation.
3. General purpose was to stabilize banking and monetary systems.
4. All national banks and some state-chartered banks belong to system.
5. Operates independently from President and with little control by Congress.
6. Ability to influence availability of money and credit is used in effort to offset economic fluctuations.

SELECTED TEST QUESTIONS

I. Multiple Choice

1. The Cabinet post which long served as a hub of political activity and patronage was:
   (a) Secretary of State; (b) Attorney General; (c) Secretary of Defense; (d) Postmaster General.
2. During most of the nineteenth century, the major source of tax revenue for the national government was:
   (a) individual income tax; (b) corporation income tax; (c) excise tax; (d) tariffs.
3. Ultimate responsibility for initiating the national budget falls on:
   (a) both houses of Congress; (b) the House Ways and Means Committee; (c) the Secretary of the Treasury; (d) the President.
4. Responsibility for auditing federal expenditures falls on the:
   (a) Treasury Department; (b) Office of Management and Budget; (c) General Accounting Office; (d) House Ways and Means Committee.
5. The portion of federal tax revenue produced by the individual income tax is:
   (a) about 10 percent; (b) about 20 percent; (c) about 40 percent; (d) about 60 percent.

II. True-False

1. The United States Comptroller General is appointed by the President with Senate approval to serve a term of 15 years.
2. Congress established the Tennessee Valley Authority in response to demands of private-power interests.
3. The Atomic Energy Act of 1946 established civilian control over the nation's program of atomic energy research and development.
4. Before the Constitution of 1787 was adopted, each state had its own currency.
5. The Federal Deposit Insurance Corporation insures deposits in national banks only.

Final Examination Essay Topics

1. Compare and contrast the basic features of these three structural forms of government, citing examples of where they were being used at the time of the U.S. Constitutional Convention in 1787:
   a. Unitary.
   b. Confederation.
   c. Federation.
2. Discuss the roles played by these three men in connection with the writing and adopting of the Constitution of 1787:
   a. James Madison.
   b. George Washington.
   c. Alexander Hamilton.
3. Compare and contrast the basic features of these two major proposals which were placed before the Philadelphia Convention:
   a. The Virginia Plan.
   b. The New Jersey Plan.
4. What were the major reasons for dissatisfaction growing out of the Articles of Confederation which inspired interest in the drafting of a new Constitution?
5. What were the predominant occupational and economic interests of the men who met in Philadelphia to draft a new Constitution?
6. It has been said that the nature of the credentials and authorizations carried by the delegates to the Constitutional Convention are such as to render the Constitution unconstitutional. Discuss.
7. If the Constitution of the United States can be described as a basic charter of government, how can the Declaration of Independence best be described?
8. Compare and contrast the Articles of Confederation with the U.S. Constitution of 1787 and tell how the governments they created compared in these respects:
   a. Executive leadership.
   b. Legislative structure.
   c. Financial stability.
   d. Supremacy, as compared with the state governments.
9. An Englishman and a Frenchman played significant roles in the move for independence and stability in the United States. Discuss the roles played by:
   a. John Locke.
   b. Baron Montesquieu.
10. Theoretically, federalism is a governmental system in which sovereignty is divided between/among two or more levels of government. How does the practice differ from the theory in the government of the United States?
11. Compare and contrast the roles of the executive in a presidential form of government and a cabinet form, paying especial attention to:
    a. Term of office.
    b. Political relationship with the legislative branch.
    c. Ability to give the people a voice in policy issues.

12. What is wrong with the statement that "Ours is a system of laws, not men"?
13. Article III of the Constitution practically assures life tenure for most federal judges. Compare the possible advantages and disadvantages of such a provision.
14. What effect did the Great Depression have on the federalist structure of government in the United States?
15. As regards freedom of religion, how does the "wall of separation" doctrine differ from the "no preference" doctrine?
16. What impact has the fourteenth amendment had on the basic structure of federalism in the United States?
17. For many years, the Bill of Rights in the United States Constitution restrained the national government only. Today it restrains states as well as the national government. Tell how this change came about.
18. Explain how the equal protection clause of the fourteenth amendment has figured in the Negro-rights movement.
19. Explain how the seniority rule in Congress affects the rural-conservative makeup of the national legislature.
20. Does freedom of the press include freedom to print lies? Discuss.
21. Courts in the United States are said to be the most powerful in the world. What is the explanation of this unusual power and its origin?
22. What are the powers and significance of the House Rules Committee?
23. It has been said that the independent regulatory commissions pose a threat to democratic values. Discuss.
24. What effect has engagement in total war had on relationships between the President and Congress?
25. Describe the structure and jurisdiction of *constitutional* courts in the federal judicial system.

APPENDIX A

Signers of the Declaration of Independence

Fifty members of the Second Continental Congress signed the engrossed copy of the Declaration on August 2, 1776; they were:

John Hancock (Mass.)
Josiah Bartlett (N.H.)
Philip Livingston (N.Y.)
Robert T. Paine (Mass.)
William Floyd (N.Y.)
John Adams (Mass.)
Francis Lewis (N.Y.)
George Walton (Ga.)
Samuel Adams (Mass.)
Richard Stockton (N.J.)
Samuel Huntington (Conn.)
Stephen Hopkins (R.I.)
John Hart (N.J.)
Abraham Clark (N.J.)
Lewis Morris (N.Y.)
John Morton (Pa.)
Francis Lightfoot Lee (Pa.)
John Penn (N.C.)
Roger Sherman (Conn.)
William Whipple (N.H.)
John Witherspoon (N.J.)
William Ellery (R.I.)
William Hooper (N.C.)
Robert Morris (Pa.)
Benjamin Harrison (Va.)

William Williams (Conn.)
Benjamin Franklin (Pa.)
William Paca (Md.)
Francis Hopkinson (N.J.)
Thomas Stone (Md.)
Charles Carroll (Md.)
Thomas Jefferson (Va.)
George Taylor (Pa.)
Edward Rutledge (S.C.)
Joseph Hewes (N.C.)
James Smith (Pa.)
George Ross (Pa.)
George Clymer (Pa.)
Thomas Hayward, Jr. (S.C.)
Button Gwinnett (Ga.)
George Read (Del.)
James Wilson (Pa.)
Thomas Lynch, Jr. (S.C.)
Samuel Chase (Md.)
Carter Braxton (Va.)
Benjamin Rush (Pa.)
Lyman Hall (Ga.)
Caesar Rodney (Del.)
Thomas Nelson (Va.)
Arthur Middleton (S.C.)

Other signers included George Wythe (Va.) who signed on August 27, and Richard Henry Lee (Va.), Elbridge Gerry (Mass.), and Oliver Wolcott (Conn.), all of whom signed on November 19. Thomas McKean (Del.) signed in 1781.

APPENDIX B

Signers of the Constitution

George Washington—Convention President and Delegate from Virginia.

CONNECTICUT

William Samuel Johnson
Roger Sherman*

DELAWARE

Richard Bassett
Gunning Bedford, Jr.
Jacob Broom
John Dickinson
George Read*

GEORGIA

Abraham Baldwin
William Few

MARYLAND

Daniel Carroll
James McHenry
Dan of St. Thomas Jenifer

MASSACHUSETTS

Nathaniel Gorham
Rufus King

NEW HAMPSHIRE

Nicholas Gilman
John Langdon

NEW YORK

Alexander Hamilton

NEW JERSEY

David Brearley
Jonathan Dayton
William Livingston
William Paterson

NORTH CAROLINA

William Blount
Richard Dobbs Spaight
Hugh Williamson

PENNSYLVANIA

George Clymer*
Thomas FitzSimons
Benjamin Franklin*
Jared Ingersoll
Thomas Mifflin
Gouverneur Morris
Robert Morris*
James Wilson*

SOUTH CAROLINA

Pierce Butler
Charles Pinckney
Charles Cotesworth Pinckney
John Rutledge

VIRGINIA

John Blair
James Madison

*Also signed the Declaration of Independence.

APPENDIX C

Constitution of the United States

Proposed by Convention September 17, 1787
Effective March 4, 1789

WE the people of the United States, in order to form a more perfect union, establish justice, insure domestic tranquility, provide for the common defense, promote the general welfare, and secure the blessings of liberty to ourselves and our posterity, do ordain and establish this Constitution for the United States of America.

ARTICLE I

SECTION 1. All legislative powers herein granted shall be vested in a Congress of the United States, which shall consist of a Senate and House of Representatives.

SECTION 2. 1. The House of Representatives shall be composed of members chosen every second year by the people of the several States, and the electors in each State shall have the qualifications requisite for electors of the most numerous branch of the State legislature.

2. No person shall be a representative who shall not have attained to the age of twenty-five years, and been seven years a citizen of the United States, and who shall not, when elected, be an inhabitant of that State in which he shall be chosen.

3. Representatives and direct taxes[1] shall be apportioned among the several States which may be included within this Union, according to their respective numbers, [which shall be determined by adding to the whole number of free persons, including those bound to service for a term of years, and excluding Indians not taxed, three fifths of all other persons.][2] The actual enumeration shall be made within three years after the first meeting of the Congress of the United States, and within every subsequent term of ten years, in such manner as they shall by law direct. The number of representatives shall not exceed one for every thirty thousand, but each State shall have at least one representative; and until such enumeration shall be made, the State of New Hampshire shall be entitled to choose three, Massachusetts eight, Rhode Island and Providence Plantations one, Connecticut five, New York six, New Jersey four, Pennsylvania eight, Delaware one, Maryland six, Virginia ten, North Carolina five, South Carolina five, and Georgia three.

4. When vacancies happen in the representation from any State, the executive authority thereof shall issue writs of election to fill such vacancies.

5. The House of Representatives shall choose their speaker and other officers; and shall have the sole power of impeachment.

SECTION 3. 1. The Senate of the United States shall be composed of two senators from each State, [chosen by the legislature thereof,][3] for six years; and each senator shall have one vote.

2. Immediately after they shall be assembled in consequence of the first election, they shall be divided as equally as may be into three classes. The seats of the senators of the first class shall be vacated at the expiration of the second year, of the second class at the expiration of the fourth year, and of the third class at the expiration of the sixth year, so that one third may be chosen every second year; and

[1]See the sixteenth amendment.
[2]See the fourteenth amendment.
[3]See the seventeenth amendment.

if vacancies happen by resignation, or otherwise, during the recess of the legislature of any State, the executive thereof may make temporary appointments until the next meeting of the legislature, which shall then fill such vacancies.[3]

3. No person shall be a senator who shall not have attained to the age of thirty years, and been nine years a citizen of the United States, and who shall not, when elected, be an inhabitant of that State for which he shall be chosen.

4. The Vice President of the United States shall be President of the Senate, but shall have no vote, unless they be equally divided.

5. The Senate shall choose their other officers, and also a president *pro tempore*, in the absence of the Vice President, or when he shall exercise the office of the President of the United States.

6. The Senate shall have the sole power to try all impeachments. When sitting for that purpose, they shall be on oath or affirmation. When the President of the United States is tried, the chief justice shall preside: and no person shall be convicted without the concurrence of two thirds of the members present.

7. Judgment in cases of impeachment shall not extend further than to removal from office, and dis-qualifications to hold and enjoy any office of honor, trust or profit under the United States: but the party convicted shall nevertheless be liable and subject to indictment, trial, judgment and punishment, according to law.

SECTION 4. 1. The times, places, and manner of holding elections for senators and representatives, shall be prescribed in each State by the legislature thereof; but the Congress may at any time by law make or alter such regulations, except as to the places of choosing senators.

2. The Congress shall assemble at least once in every year, and such meeting shall be on the first Monday in December,[4] unless they shall by law appoint a different day.

SECTION 5. 1. Each House shall be the judge of the elections, returns and qualifications of its own members, and a majority of each shall constitute a quorum to do business; but a smaller number may adjourn from day to day, and may be authorized to compel the attendance of absent members, in such manner, and under such penalties as each House may provide.

2. Each House may determine the rules of its proceedings, punish its members for disorderly be-havior, and, with the concurrence of two thirds, expel a member.

3. Each House shall keep a journal of its proceedings, and from time to time publish the same, ex-cepting such parts as may in their judgment require secrecy; and the yeas and nays of the members of either House on any question shall, at the desire of one fifth of those present, be entered on the journal.

4. Neither House, during the session of Congress, shall, without the consent of the other, adjourn for more than three days, nor to any other place than that in which the two Houses shall be sitting.

SECTION 6. 1. The senators and representatives shall receive a compensation for their services, to be ascertained by law, and paid out of the Treasury of the United States. They shall in all cases, except treason, felony, and breach of the peace, be privileged from arrest during their attendance at the ses-sion of their respective Houses, and in going to and returning from the same; and for any speech or debate in either House, they shall not be questioned in any other place.

2. No senator or representative shall, during the time for which he was elected, be appointed to any civil office under the authority of the United States, which shall have been created, or the emoluments whereof shall have been increased during such time; and no person holding any office under the United States shall be a member of either House during his continuance in office.

SECTION 7. 1. All bills for raising revenue shall originate in the House of Representatives; but the Senate may propose or concur with amendments as on other bills.

[3]See the seventeenth amendment.
[4]Modified by the twentieth amendment.

2. Every bill which shall have passed the House of Representatives and the Senate, shall, before it becomes a law, be presented to the President of the United States; if he approves he shall sign it, but if not he shall return it, with his objections to that House in which it shall have originated, who shall enter the objections at large on their journal, and proceed to reconsider it. If after such reconsideration two thirds of that House shall agree to pass the bill, it shall be sent, together with the objections, to the other House, by which it shall likewise be reconsidered, and if approved by two thirds of that House, it shall become a law. But in all such cases the votes of both Houses shall be determined by yeas and nays, and the names of the persons voting for and against the bill shall be entered on the journal of each House respectively. If any bill shall not be returned by the President within ten days (Sundays excepted) after it shall have been presented to him, the same shall be a law, in like manner as if he had signed it, unless the Congress by their adjournment prevent its return, in which case it shall not be a law.

3. Every order, resolution, or vote to which the concurrence of the Senate and the House of Representatives may be necessary (except on a question of adjournment) shall be presented to the President of the United States; and before the same shall take effect, shall be approved by him, or being disapproved by him, shall be repassed by two thirds of the Senate and House of Representatives, according to the rules and limitations prescribed in the case of a bill.

SECTION 8. The Congress shall have the power

1. To lay and collect taxes, duties, imposts, and excises, to pay the debts and provide for the common defense and general welfare of the United States; but all duties, imposts, and excises shall be uniform throughout the United States;

2. To borrow money on the credit of the United States;

3. To regulate commerce with foreign nations, and among the several States, and with the Indian tribes;

4. To establish a uniform rule of naturalization, and uniform laws on the subject of bankruptcies throughout the United States;

5. To coin money, regulate the value thereof, and of foreign coin, and fix the standard of weights and measures;

6. To provide for the punishment of counterfeiting the securities and current coin of the United States;

7. To establish post offices and post roads;

8. To promote the progress of science and useful arts, by securing for limited times to authors and inventors the exclusive right to their respective writings and discoveries;

9. To constitute tribunals inferior to the Supreme Court;

10. To define and punish piracies and felonies committed on the high seas, and offenses against the law of nations;

11. To declare war, grant letters of marque and reprisal, and make rules concerning captures on land and water;

12. To raise and support armies, but no appropriation of money to that use shall be for a longer term than two years;

13. To provide and maintain a navy;

14. To make rules for the government and regulation of the land and naval forces;

15. To provide for calling forth the militia to execute the laws of the Union, suppress insurrections and repel invasions;

16. To provide for organizing, arming, and disciplining the militia, and for governing such part of them as may be employed in the service of the United States, reserving to the States respectively, the appointment of the officers, and the authority of training the militia according to the discipline prescribed by Congress;

17. To exercise exclusive legislation in all cases whatsoever, over such district (not exceeding ten miles square) as may, by cession of particular States, and the acceptance of Congress, become the seat of the government of the United States, and to exercise like authority over all places purchased by the consent of the legislature of the State in which the same shall be, for the erection of forts, magazines, arsenals, dockyards, and other useful buildings; and

18. To make all laws which shall be necessary and proper for carrying into execution the foregoing powers, and all other powers vested by this Constitution in the government of the United States, or in any department or officer thereof.

SECTION 9. 1. The migration or importation of such persons as any of the States now existing shall think proper to admit, shall not be prohibited by the Congress prior to the year one thousand eight hundred and eight, but a tax or duty may be imposed on such importation, not exceeding ten dollars for each person.

2. The privilege of the writ of *habeas corpus* shall not be suspended, unless when in cases of rebellion or invasion the public safety may require it.

3. No bill of attainder or *ex post facto* law shall be passed.

4. No capitation, or other direct, tax shall be laid, unless in proportion to the census or enumeration hereinbefore directed to be taken.[5]

5. No tax or duty shall be laid on articles exported from any State.

6. No preference shall be given by any regulation of commerce or revenue to the ports of one State over those of another: nor shall vessels bound to, or from, one State be obliged to enter, clear, or pay duties in another.

7. No money shall be drawn from the treasury, but in consequence of appropriations made by law; and a regular statement and account of the receipts and expenditures of all public money shall be published from time to time.

8. No title of nobility shall be granted by the United States: and no person holding any office of profit or trust under them, shall, without the consent of the Congress, accept of any present, emolument, office, or title, of any kind whatever, from any king, prince, or foreign State.

SECTION 10. 1. No State shall enter into any treaty, alliance, or confederation; grant letters of marque and reprisal; coin money; emit bills of credit; make anything but gold and silver coin a tender in payment of debts; pass any bill of attainder, *ex post facto* law, or law impairing the obligation of contracts, or grant any title of nobility.

2. No State shall, without the consent of the Congress, lay any imposts or duties on imports or exports, except what may be absolutely necessary for executing its inspection laws; and the net produce of all duties and imposts laid by any State on imports or exports, shall be for the use of the treasury of the United States; and all such laws shall be subject to the revision and control of the Congress.

3. No State shall, without the consent of the Congress, lay any duty of tonnage, keep troops, or ships of war in time of peace, enter into any agreement or compact with another State, or with a foreign power, or engage in war, unless actually invaded, or in such imminent danger as will not admit of delay.

ARTICLE II

SECTION 1. 1. The executive power shall be vested in a President of the United States of America. He shall hold his office during the term of four years, and, together with the Vice President, chosen for the same term, be elected as follows:

2. Each State[6] shall appoint, in such manner as the legislature thereof may direct, a number of electors, equal to the whole number of senators and representatives to which the State may be entitled in the Congress: but no senator or representative, or person holding an office of trust or profit under the United States, shall be appointed an elector.

[5]See the sixteenth amendment.
[6]See twenty-third amendment.

The electors shall meet in their respective States, and vote by ballot for two persons, of whom one at least shall not be an inhabitant of the same State with themselves. And they shall make a list of all the persons voted for, and of the number of votes for each; which list they shall sign and certify, and transmit sealed to the seat of the government of the United States, directed to the president of the Senate. The president of the Senate shall, in the presence of the Senate and House of Representatives, open all the certificates, and the votes shall then be counted. The person having the greatest number of votes shall be the President, if such number be a majority of the whole number of electors appointed; and if there be more than one who have such a majority, and have an equal number of votes, then the House of Representatives shall immediately choose by ballot one of them for President; and if no person have a majority, then from the five highest on the list the said House shall in like manner choose the President. But in choosing the President, the votes shall be taken by States, the representation from each State having one vote; a quorum for this purpose shall consist of a member or members from two thirds of the States, and a majority of all the States shall be necessary to a choice. In every case, after the choice of the President, the person having the greatest number of votes of the electors shall be the Vice President. But if there should remain two or more who have equal votes, the Senate shall choose from them by ballot the Vice President.[7]

3. The Congress may determine the time of choosing the electors, and the day on which they shall give their votes; which day shall be the same throughout the United States.

4. No person except a natural born citizen, or a citizen of the United States, at the time of the adoption of this Constitution, shall be eligible to the office of President; neither shall any person be eligible to that office who shall not have attained to the age of thirty-five years, and been fourteen years a resident within the United States.

5. In case of the removal of the President from office, or of his death, resignation, or inability to discharge the powers and duties of the said office, the same shall devolve on the Vice President, and the Congress may by law provide for the case of removal, death, resignation, or inability, both of the President and Vice President, declaring what officer shall then act as President, and such officer shall act accordingly, until the disability be removed, or a President shall be elected.

6. The President shall, at stated times, receive for his services a compensation, which shall neither be increased nor diminished during the period for which he shall have been elected, and he shall not receive within that period any other emolument from the United States, or any of them.

7. Before he enter on the execution of his office, he shall take the following oath or affirmation: — "I do solemnly swear (or affirm) that I will faithfully execute the office of President of the United States, and will to the best of my ability, preserve, protect and defend the Constitution of the United States."

SECTION 2. 1. The President shall be commander in chief of the army and navy of the United States, and of the militia of the several States, when called into the actual service of the United States; he may require the opinion, in writing, of the principal officer in each of the executive departments, upon any subject relating to the duties of their respective offices, and he shall have power to grant reprieves and pardons for offenses against the United States, except in cases of impeachment.

2. He shall have power, by and with the advice and consent of the Senate, to make treaties, provided two thirds of the senators present concur; and he shall nominate, and by and with the advice and consent of the Senate, shall appoint ambassadors, other public ministers and consuls, judges of the Supreme Court, and all other officers of the United States, whose appointments are not herein otherwise provided for, and which shall be established by law: but the Congress may by law vest the appointment of such inferior officers, as they think proper, in the President alone, in the courts of law, or in the heads of departments.

3. The President shall have power to fill up all vacancies that may happen during the recess of the Senate, by granting commissions which shall expire at the end of their next session.

---

[7]This paragraph was superseded by the twelfth amendment.

SECTION 3. He shall from time to time give to the Congress information of the state of the Union, and recommend to their consideration such measures as he shall judge necessary and expedient; he may, on extraordinary occasions, convene both Houses, or either of them, and in case of disagreement between them with respect to the time of adjournment, he may adjourn them to such time as he shall think proper; he shall receive ambassadors and other public ministers; he shall take care that the laws be faithfully executed, and shall commission all the officers of the United States.

SECTION 4. The President, Vice President, and all civil officers of the United States, shall be removed from office on impeachment for, and conviction of, treason, bribery, or other high crimes and and misdemeanors.

ARTICLE III

SECTION 1. The judicial power of the United States shall be vested in one Supreme Court, and in such inferior courts as the Congress may from time to time ordain and establish. The judges, both of the Supreme and inferior courts, shall hold their offices during good behavior, and shall, at stated times, receive for their services, a compensation, which shall not be diminished during their continuance in office.

SECTION 2. 1. The judicial power shall extend to all cases, in law and equity, arising under this Constitution, the laws of the United States, and treaties made, or which shall be made, under their authority;—to all cases affecting ambassadors, other public ministers and consuls;—to all cases of admiralty and maritime jurisdiction;—to controversies to which the United States shall be a party;—to controversies between two or more States;—between a State and citizens of another State;[8]—between citizens of different States;—between citizens of the same State claiming lands under grants of different States, and [between a State], or the citizens thereof, and [foreign] States, [citizens or subjects.][8]

2. In all cases affecting ambassadors, other public ministers and consuls, and those in which a State shall be party, the Supreme Court shall have original jurisdiction. In all the other cases before mentioned, the Supreme Court shall have appellate jurisdiction, both as to law and to fact, with such exceptions, and under such regulations as the Congress shall make.

3. The trial of all crimes, except in cases of impeachment, shall be by jury; and such trial shall be held in the State where the said crimes shall have been committed; but when not committed within any State, the trial shall be at such place or places as the Congress may by law have directed.

SECTION 3. 1. Treason against the United States shall consist only in levying war against them, or in adhering to their enemies, giving them aid and comfort. No person shall be convicted of treason unless on the testimony of two witnesses to the same overt act, or on confession in open court.

2. The Congress shall have power to declare the punishment of treason, but no attainder of treason shall work corruption of blood, or forfeiture except during the life of the person attained.

ARTICLE IV

SECTION 1. Full faith and credit shall be given in each State to the public acts, records, and judicial proceedings of every other State. And the Congress may by general laws prescribe the manner in which such acts, records and proceedings shall be proved, and the effect thereof.

SECTION 2. 1. The citizens of each State shall be entitled to all privileges and immunities of citizens in the several States.[9]

2. A person charged in any State with treason, felony, or other crime, who shall flee from justice, and be found in another State, shall on demand of the executive authority of the State from which he fled, be delivered up to be removed to the State having jurisdiction of the crime.

[8]See the eleventh amendment.
[9]See the fourteenth amendment, section 1.

3. No person held to service or labor in one State under the laws thereof, escaping into another, shall, in consequence of any law or regulation therein, be discharged from such service or labor, but shall be delivered up on claim of the party to whom such service or labor may be due.[10]

SECTION 3. 1. New States may be admitted by the Congress into this Union; but no new State shall be formed or erected within the jurisdiction of any other State; nor any State be formed by the junction of two or more States, or parts of States, without the consent of the legislatures of the States concerned as well as of the Congress.

2. The Congress shall have power to dispose of and make all needful rules and regulations respecting the territory or other property belonging to the United States; and nothing in this Constitution shall be so construed as to prejudice any claims of the United States, or of any particular State.

SECTION 4. The United States shall guarantee to every State in this Union a republican form of government, and shall protect each of them against invasion; and on application of the legislature, or of the executive (when the legislature cannot be convened) against domestic violence.

ARTICLE V

The Congress, whenever two thirds of both Houses shall deem it necessary, shall propose amendments to this Constitution, or, on the application of the legislatures of two thirds of the several States, shall call a convention for proposing amendments, which in either case, shall be valid to all intents and purposes, as part of this Constitution when ratified by the legislatures of three fourths of the several States, or by conventions in three fourths thereof, as the one or the other mode of ratification may be proposed by the Congress; Provided that no amendment which may be made prior to the year one thousand eight hundred and eight shall in any manner affect the first and fourth clauses in the ninth section of the first article; and that no State, without its consent, shall be deprived of its equal suffrage in the Senate.

ARTICLE VI

1. All debts contracted and engagements entered into, before the adoption of this Constitution, shall be as valid against the United States under this Constitution, as under the Confederation.

2. This Constitution, and the laws of the United States which shall be made in pursuance thereof; and all treaties made, or which shall be made, under the authority of the United States, shall be the supreme law of the land; and the Judges in every State shall be bound thereby, anything in the Constitution or laws of any State to the contrary notwithstanding.

3. The senators and representatives before mentioned, and the members of the several State legislatures, and all executive and judicial officers, both of the United States and of the several States, shall be bound by oath or affirmation to support this Constitution; but no religious test shall ever be required as a qualification to any office or public trust under the United States.

ARTICLE VII

The ratification of the conventions of nine States shall be sufficient for the establishment of this Constitution between the States so ratifying the same.

Done in Convention by the unanimous consent of the States present the seventeenth day of September in the year of our Lord one thousand seven hundred and eighty-seven, and of the independence of United States of America the twelfth. In witness whereof we have hereunto subscribed our names. [Names omitted]

[10]See the thirteenth amendment.

Articles in addition to, and amendment of, the Constitution of the United States of America, proposed by Congress, and ratified by the legislatures of the several States pursuant to the fifth article of the original Constitution.

AMENDMENTS

First Ten Amendments passed by Congress September 25, 1789.
Ratified by three-fourths of the States December 15, 1791.

ARTICLE I

Congress shall make no law respecting an establishment of religion, or prohibiting the free exercise thereof; or abridging the freedom of speech, or of the press; or the right of the people peaceably to assemble, and to petition the government for a redress of grievances.

ARTICLE II

A well regulated militia, being necessary to the security of a free State, the right of the people to keep and bear arms, shall not be infringed.

ARTICLE III

No soldier shall, in time of peace be quartered in any house, without the consent of the owner, nor in time of war, but in a manner to be prescribed by law.

ARTICLE IV

The right of the people to be secure in their persons, houses, papers, and effects, against unreasonable searches and seizures, shall not be violated, and no warrants shall issue, but upon probable cause, supported by oath or affirmation, and particularly describing the place to be searched, and the persons or things to be seized.

ARTICLE V

No person shall be held to answer for a capital, or otherwise infamous crime, unless on a presentment or indictment of a grand jury, except in cases arising in the land or naval forces, or in the militia, when in actual service in time of war or public danger; nor shall any person be subject for the same offense to be twice put in jeopardy of life or limb; nor shall be compelled in any criminal case to be a witness against himself, nor be deprived of life, liberty, or property, without due process of law; nor shall private property be taken for public use without just compensation.

ARTICLE VI

In all criminal prosecutions, the accused shall enjoy the right to a speedy and public trial, by an impartial jury of the State and district wherein the crime shall have been committed, which district shall have been previously ascertained by law, and to be informed of the nature and cause of the accusation; to be confronted with the witnesses against him; to have compulsory process for obtaining witnesses in his favor, and to have the assistance of counsel for his defense.

ARTICLE VII

In suits at common law, where the value in controversy shall exceed twenty dollars, the right of trial by jury shall be preserved, and no fact tried by a jury shall be otherwise reëxamined in any court of the United States, than according to the rules of the common law.

ARTICLE VIII

Excessive bail shall not be required, nor excessive fines imposed, nor cruel and unusual punishments inflicted.

ARTICLE IX

The enumeration in the Constitution of certain rights shall not be construed to deny or disparage others retained by the people.

ARTICLE X

The powers not delegated to the United States by the Constitution, nor prohibited by it to the States, are reserved to the States respectively, or to the people.

ARTICLE XI

Passed by Congress March 4, 1794. Ratified February 7, 1795.

The judicial power of the United States shall not be construed to extend to any suit in law or equity, commenced or prosecuted against one of the United States by citizens of another State, or by citizens or subjects of any foreign State.

ARTICLE XII

Passed by Congress December 9, 1803. Ratified July 27, 1804.

The electors shall meet in their respective States, and vote by ballot for President and Vice President, one of whom, at least, shall not be an inhabitant of the same State with themselves; they shall name in their ballots the person voted for as President, and in distinct ballots, the person voted for as Vice President, and they shall make distinct lists of all persons voted for as President and of all persons voted for as Vice President, and of the number of votes for each, which lists they shall sign and certify, and transmit sealed to the seat of the government of the United States, directed to the President of the Senate;—The President of the Senate shall, in the presence of the Senate and House of Representatives, open all the certificates and the votes shall then be counted;—The person having the greatest number of votes for President, shall be the President, if such number be a majority of the whole number of electors appointed; and if no person have such majority, then from the persons having the highest numbers not exceeding three on the list of those voted for as President, the House of Representatives shall choose immediately, by ballot, the President. But in choosing the President, the votes shall be taken by States, the representation from each State having one vote; a quorum for this purpose shall consist of a member or members from two thirds of the States, and a majority of all the States shall be necessary to a choice. And if the House of Representatives shall not choose a President whenever the right of choice shall devolve upon them, before the fourth day of March[11] next following, then the Vice President shall act as President, as in the case of the death or other constitutional disability of the President. The person having the greatest number of votes as Vice President shall be the Vice President, if such number be a majority of the whole number of electors appointed, and if no person have a majority, then from the two highest numbers on the list, the Senate shall choose the Vice President; a quorum for the purpose shall consist of two thirds of the whole number of Senators, and a majority of the whole number shall be necessary to a choice. But no person constitutionally ineligible to the office of President shall be eligible to that of Vice President of the United States.

[11]See twentieth amendment.

ARTICLE XIII
Passed by Congress January 31, 1865. Ratified December 6, 1865.

SECTION 1. Neither slavery nor involuntary servitude, except as punishment for crime whereof the party shall have been duly convicted, shall exist within the United States, or any place subject to their jurisdiction.

SECTION 2. Congress shall have power to enforce this article by appropriate legislation.

ARTICLE XIV
Passed by Congress June 13, 1866. Ratified July 9, 1868.

SECTION 1. All persons born or naturalized in the United States, and subject to the jurisdiction thereof, are citizens of the United States and of the State wherein they reside. No State shall make or enforce any law which shall abridge the privileges or immunities of citizens of the United States; nor shall any State deprive any person of life, liberty, or property, without due process of law; nor deny to any person within its jurisdiction the equal protection of the laws.

SECTION 2. Representatives shall be apportioned among the several States according to their respective numbers, counting the whole number of persons in each State, excluding Indians not taxed. But when the right to vote at any election for the choice of electors for President and Vice President of the United States, representatives in Congress, the executive and judicial officers of a State, or the members of the legislature thereof, is denied to any of the male inhabitants of such State, being twenty-one years of age, and citizens of the United States, or in any way abridged, except for participation in rebellion, or other crime, the basis of representation therein shall be reduced in the proportion which the number of such male citizens shall bear to the whole number of male citizens twenty-one years of age in such State.

SECTION 3. No person shall be a senator or representative in Congress, or elector of President and Vice President, or hold any office, civil or military, under the United States, or under any State, who having previously taken an oath, as a member of Congress, or as an officer of the United States, or as a member of any State legislature, or as an executive or judicial officer of any State, to support the Constitution of the United States, shall have engaged in insurrection or rebellion against the same, or given aid or comfort to the enemies thereof. But Congress may by a vote of two thirds of each House, remove such disability.

SECTION 4. The validity of the public debt of the United States, authorized by law, including debts incurred for payment of pensions and bounties for services in suppressing insurrection or rebellion, shall not be questioned. But neither the United States nor any State shall assume or pay any debt or obligation incurred in aid of insurrection or rebellion against the United States, or any claim for the loss or emancipation of any slave; but all such debts, obligations, and claims shall be held illegal and void.

SECTION 5. The Congress shall have power to enforce, by appropriate legislation, the provisions of this article.

ARTICLE XV
Passed by Congress February 26, 1869. Ratified February 3, 1870.

SECTION 1. The right of citizens of the United States to vote shall not be denied or abridged by the United States or by any State on account of race, color, or previous condition of servitude.

SECTION 2. The Congress shall have power to enforce this article by appropriate legislation.

ARTICLE XVI
Passed by Congress July 2, 1909. Ratified February 3, 1913.

The Congress shall have power to lay and collect taxes on incomes, from whatever source derived, with apportionment among the several States, and without regard to any census or enumeration.

ARTICLE XVII
Passed by Congress May 13, 1912. Ratified April 8, 1913.

The Senate of the United States shall be composed of two senators from each state, elected by the people thereof, for six years; and each senator shall have one vote. The electors in each State shall have the qualifications requisite for electors of the most numerous branch of the State legislature.

When vacancies happen in the representation of any State in the Senate, the executive authority of such State shall issue writs of election to fill such vacancies: *Provided,* That the legislature of any State may empower the executive thereof to make temporary appointments until the people fill the vacancies by election as the legislature may direct.

This amendment shall not be so construed as to affect the election or term of any senator chosen before it becomes valid as part of the Constitution.

ARTICLE XVIII[12]
Passed by Congress December 18, 1917. Ratified January 16, 1919.

After one year from the ratification of this article, the manufacture, sale, or transportation of intoxicating liquors within, the importation thereof into, or the exportation thereof from the United States and all territory subject to the jurisdiction thereof for beverage purposes is hereby prohibited.

The Congress and the several States shall have concurrent power to enforce this article by appropriate legislation.

This article shall be inoperative unless it shall have been ratified as an amendment to the Constitution by the legislatures of the several States, as provided in the Constitution, within seven years from the date of the submission hereof to the States by Congress.

ARTICLE XIX
Passed by Congress June 4, 1919. Ratified August 18, 1920.

The right of citizens of the United States to vote shall not be denied or abridged by the United States or by any State on account of sex.

The Congress shall have power by appropriate legislation to enforce the provisions of this article.

ARTICLE XX
Passed by Congress March 2, 1932. Ratified January 23, 1933.

SECTION 1. The terms of the President and Vice President shall end at noon on the 20th day of January, and the terms of Senators and Representatives at noon on the 3d day of January, of the years in which such terms would have ended if this article had not been ratified; and the terms of their successors shall then begin.

SECTION 2. The Congress shall assemble at least once in every year, and such meeting shall begin at noon on the 3rd day of January, unless they shall by law appoint a different day.

SECTION 3. If, at the time fixed for the beginning of the term of the President, the President-elect shall have died, the Vice President-elect shall become President. If a President shall not have been chosen before the time fixed for the beginning of his term, or if the President-elect shall have failed to qualify, then the Vice President-elect shall act as President until a President shall have qualified; and the Congress may by law provide for the case wherein neither a President-elect nor a Vice President-elect shall have qualified, declaring who shall then act as President, or the manner in which one who is to act shall be selected, and such person shall act accordingly until a President or Vice President shall have qualified.

[12]Repealed by the twenty-first amendment.

SECTION 4. The Congress may by law provide for the case of the death of any of the persons from whom the House of Representatives may choose a President whenever the right of choice shall have devolved upon them, and for the case of the death of any of the persons from whom the Senate may choose a Vice President whenever the right of choice shall have devolved upon them.

SECTION 5. Sections 1 and 2 shall take effect on the 15th day of October following the ratification of this article.

SECTION 6. This article shall be inoperative unless it shall have been ratified as an amendment to the Constitution by the legislatures of three-fourths of the several States within seven years from the date of its submission.

ARTICLE XXI
Passed by Congress February 20, 1933. Ratified December 5, 1933.

SECTION 1. The Eighteenth Article of amendment to the Constitution of the United States is hereby repealed.

SECTION 2. The transportation or importation into any State, Territory, or possession of the United States for delivery or use therein of intoxicating liquors in violation of the laws thereof, is hereby prohibited.

SECTION 3. This article shall be inoperative unless it shall have been ratified as an amendment to the Constitution by conventions in the several States, as provided in the Constitution, within seven years from the date of the submission thereof to the States by the Congress.

ARTICLE XXII
Passed by Congress March 21, 1947. Ratified February 27, 1951.

No person shall be elected to the office of the President more than twice, and no person who has held the office of President, or acted as President, for more than two years of a term to which some other person was elected President shall be elected to the office of the President more than once.

But this article shall not apply to any person holding the office of President when this article was proposed by the Congress, and shall not prevent any person who may be holding the office of President, or acting as President, during the term within which this article becomes operative from holding the office of President or acting as President during the remainder of such term.

This article shall be inoperative unless it shall have been ratified as an amendment to the Constitution by the legislatures of three-fourths of the several states within seven years from the date of its submission to the states by the Congress.

ARTICLE XXIII
Passed by Congress June 16, 1960. Ratified March 29, 1961.

SECTION 1. The District constituting the seat of Government of the United States shall appoint in such manner as the Congress may direct:

A number of electors of President and Vice President equal to the whole number of Senators and Representatives in Congress to which the District would be entitled if it were a State, but in no event more than the least populous state; they shall be in addition to those appointed by the states, but shall be considered, for the purpose of the election of President and Vice President, to be electors appointed by a state; and they shall meet in the District and perform such duties as provided by the twelfth article of amendment.

SECTION 2. The Congress shall have power to enforce this article by appropriate legislation.

ARTICLE XXIV

Passed by Congress August 27, 1962. Ratified January 23, 1964.

SECTION 1. The right of citizens of the United States to vote in any primary or other election for President or Vice President, for electors for President or Vice President, or for Senator or Representative in Congress, shall not be denied or abridged by the United States or any State by reason of failure to pay any poll tax or other tax.

SECTION 2. The Congress shall have the power to enforce this article by appropriate legislation.

ARTICLE XXV

Passed by Congress July 6, 1965. Ratified February 10, 1967.

SECTION 1. In case of the removal of the President from office or his death or resignation, the Vice President shall become President.

SECTION 2. Whenever there is a vacancy in the office of the Vice President, the President shall nominate a Vice President who shall take the office upon confirmation by a majority vote of both houses of Congress.

SECTION 3. Whenever the President transmits to the President pro tempore of the Senate and the Speaker of the House of Representatives his written declaration that he is unable to discharge the powers and duties of his office, and until he transmits to them a written declaration to the contrary, such powers and duties shall be discharged by the Vice President as Acting President.

SECTION 4. Whenever the Vice President and a majority of either the principal officers of the executive departments, or of such other body as Congress may by law provide, transmit to the President pro tempore of the Senate and the Speaker of the House of Representatives their written declaration that the President is unable to discharge the powers and duties of his office, the Vice President shall immediately assume the powers and duties of the office as Acting President.

Thereafter, when the President transmits to the President pro tempore of the Senate and the Speaker of the House of Representatives his written declaration that no inability exists, he shall resume the powers and duties of his office unless the Vice President and a majority of either the principal officers of the executive department, or of such other body as Congress may by law provide, transmit within four days to the President pro tempore of the Senate and the Speaker of the House of Representatives their written declaration that the President is unable to discharge the power and duties of his office. Thereupon Congress shall decide the issue, assembling within 48 hours for that purpose if not in session. If the Congress, within 21 days after receipt of the latter written declaration, or, if Congress is not in session, within 21 days after Congress is required to assemble, determines by two-thirds vote of both houses that the President is unable to discharge the powers and duties of his office, the Vice President shall continue to discharge the same as Acting President; otherwise, the President shall resume the powers and duties of his office.

ARTICLE XXVI

Ratified June 10, 1971.

SECTION 1. The right of citizens of the United States, who are eighteen years of age or older, to vote shall not be denied or abridged by the United States or by any State on account of age.

SECTION 2. The Congress shall have the power to enforce this article by appropriate legislation.

The U.S. Constitution in Brief

PREAMBLE

States the source of authority of the new government as being "We the people."

ARTICLE I

Vests all legislative authority in a bicameral Congress, lists powers and some restraints. Places some restraints on states. Lists qualifications for congressional membership.

ARTICLE II

Creates the new Executive Department, outlines powers and qualifications.

ARTICLE III

Creates the U.S. Supreme Court, authorizes Congress to create other courts, provides life tenure for judges, defines treason.

ARTICLE IV

Prescribes relation of states to each other and to the national government. Assurances to states. Government of territories.

ARTICLE V

Outlines methods for amending the Constitution. Guarantees equal representation of states in U.S. Senate.

ARTICLE VI

Guarantees payment of debts of the Confederation. Provides for supremacy of federal government. National and state officials must pledge to uphold Constitution. Religious tests for public office banned.

ARTICLE VII

Procedure for ratification of the Constitution.

AMENDMENTS

I. Freedom of religion, speech, press, assembly.
II. Right to keep and bear arms.
III. Forbids quartering soldiers in private homes.
IV. Bans unwarranted searches and seizures.
V. Protects personal and property rights. Assures procedural rights to the accused.
VI. Assures speedy trial, fairly conducted in public.
VII. Provides jury trial in civil cases.
VIII. Prohibits excessive bail and cruel punishment.
IX. People have rights other than those enumerated.
X. Undelegated powers remain with the states.
XI. States exempted from suits by citizens of other states.

XII. Revises presidential election procedure of Article I.

XIII. Abolishes slavery.

XIV. Defines citizenship. Assures due process and equal protection of law by state governments. Protects privileges and immunities of citizens against infringement by states.

XV. Adult male citizens not to be denied right to vote.

XVI. Authorizes Congress to levy income tax.

XVII. U.S. Senators to be popularly elected.

XVIII. Prohibition on intoxicating beverages.

XIX. Voting rights for women.

XX. Alters terms of President and congressmen, ends "lame duck" sessions of Congress.

XXI. Repeals eighteenth amendment.

XXII. Limits President's term of office.

XXIII. Presidential vote for District of Columbia residents.

XIV. Bans poll tax in election of national officers.

XXV. Vice President to become President when President cannot perform his duties.

XXVI. Lowers minimum voting age to eighteen.

Answers to Selected Test Questions

CHAPTER 1
I. Multiple Choice
1. a   4. d
2. b   5. a
3. d
II. True-False
1. F   4. T
2. F   5. T
3. F

CHAPTER 2
I. Multiple Choice
1. d   4. c
2. a   5. d
3. b
II. True-False
1. F   4. T
2. T   5. F
3. F

CHAPTER 3
I. Multiple Choice
1. b   4. d
2. a   5. c
3. d
II. True-False
1. T   4. T
2. F   5. T
3. T

CHAPTER 4
I. Multiple Choice
1. d   4. b
2. a   5. c
3. d
II. True-False
1. T   4. T
2. F   5. F
3. F

CHAPTER 5
I. Multiple Choice
1. d   4. a
2. c   5. d
3. c
II. True-False
1. T   4. F
2. T   5. F
3. T

CHAPTER 6
I. Multiple Choice
1. d   4. c
2. d   5. a
3. b

II. True-False
1. F   4. T
2. F   5. F
3. F

CHAPTER 7
I. Multiple Choice
1. d   4. b
2. c   5. c
3. b
II. True-False
1. T   4. F
2. F   5. F
3. F

CHAPTER 8
I. Multiple Choice
1. b   4. a
2. c   5. b
3. b
II. True-False
1. F   4. T
2. T   5. F
3. T

CHAPTER 9
I. Multiple Choice
1. a   4. a
2. b   5. c
3. d
II. True-False
1. T   4. F
2. T   5. F
3. F

CHAPTER 10
I. Multiple Choice
1. a   4. c
2. a   5. c
3. b
II. True-False
1. F   4. T
2. F   5. T
3. F

CHAPTER 11
I. Multiple Choice
1. b   4. b
2. b   5. a
3. d
II. True-False
1. T   4. T
2. T   5. F
3. T

CHAPTER 12
I. Multiple Choice
1. b   4. c
2. a   5. b
3. a
II. True-False
1. F   4. T
2. T   5. T
3. T

CHAPTER 13
I. Multiple Choice
1. a   4. d
2. b   5. c
3. c
II. True-False
1. T   4. T
2. T   5. F
3. F

CHAPTER 14
I. Multiple Choice
1. a   4. a
2. b   5. d
3. d
II. True-False
1. T   4. F
2. T   5. T
3. F

CHAPTER 15
I. Multiple Choice
1. c   4. b
2. d   5. a
3. a
II. True-False
1. F   4. F
2. T   5. F
3. T

CHAPTER 16
I. Multiple Choice
1. c   4. b
2. b   5. a
3. a
II. True-False
1. F   4. F
2. T   5. T
3. F

CHAPTER 17
I. Multiple Choice
1. b   4. d
2. a   5. d
3. b

CHAPTER 18
I. Multiple Choice
1. d   4. a
2. d   5. c
3. b
II. True-False
1. T   4. F
2. T   5. T
3. F

CHAPTER 19
I. Multiple Choice
1. a   4. d
2. b   5. a
3. c
II. True-False
1. T   4. F
2. F   5. T
3. T

CHAPTER 20
I. Multiple Choice
1. d   4. d
2. d   5. d
3. d
II. True-False
1. T   4. T
2. F   5. T
3. F

CHAPTER 21
I. Multiple Choice
1. b   4. a
2. c   5. d
3. d
II. True-False
1. T   4. F
2. F   5. T
3. T

CHAPTER 22
I. Multiple Choice
1. a   4. c
2. b   5. b
3. b
II. True-False
1. F   4. T
2. T   5. T
3. T

CHAPTER 23
I. Multiple Choice
1. a   4. b
2. b   5. d
3. c
II. True-False
1. T   4. F
2. T   5. F
3. F

CHAPTER 24
I. Multiple Choice
1. a   4. d
2. d   5. b
3. d
II. True-False
1. F   4. F
2. F   5. T
3. F

CHAPTER 25
I. Multiple Choice
1. d   4. c
2. d   5. c
3. d
II. True-False
1. T   4. T
2. F   5. F
3. T

Index

NOTES

NOTES

NOTES

NOTES

NOTES